50 Years of Philosophy of Education
Progress and Prospects

50 Years of Philosophy of Education

Progress and Prospects

Edited by
Graham Haydon

Bedford Way Papers

INSTITUTE OF
EDUCATION
UNIVERSITY OF LONDON

First published in 1998 by the Institute of Education University of London,
20 Bedford Way, London WC1H 0AL

Pursuing Excellence in Education

© Institute of Education University of London 1998

British Library Cataloguing in Publication Data;
a catalogue record for this publication is available from the British Library

ISBN 0 85473 560 7

Design and Typography by Joan Rose

Produced by Reprographic Services
Institute of Education
20 Bedford Way
London WC1H 0AL

Printed by Formara Limited
16 The Candlemakers, Temple Farm Industrial Estate
Southend on Sea, Essex SS2 5RX

October 1998

Contents

Preface
Professor Peter Mortimore   vii

Introduction   xi
Graham Haydon

1. Philosophy of Education: The Evolution of a Discipline   1
Paul H. Hirst

2. Educational Philosophies and Cultures of Philosophy   23
David E. Cooper

3. De-moralizing Education   41
Susan Mendus

4. Educational Research: Re-establishing the Philosophical Terrain   59
David Bridges

Contributors

David Bridges, Professor of Education and Pro-Vice-Chancellor, University of East Anglia

David E. Cooper, Professor of Philosophy, University of Durham

Graham Haydon, Lecturer in Philosophy of Education, Institute of Education, London.

Paul H. Hirst, Emeritus Professor of Education, University of Cambridge, and Visiting Professorial Fellow, Institute of Education, London.

Susan Mendus, Professor of Politics, University of York

Preface

Professor Peter Mortimore

This volume presents the text of four lectures which were given at the Institute of Education, University of London, in the autumn of 1997, in a series jointly sponsored by the Institute and the Philosophy of Education Society of Great Britain, to mark the fiftieth anniversary of the founding in 1947 of the established chair in Philosophy of Education at the Institute.

The association between the Institute and philosophical ideas in education has been a long one. A number of the earlier Directors of the Institute have written about the fundamental ideas that underpin our education system, from Percy Nunn's *Education: its Data and First Principles* in 1920 to William Taylor and Denis Lawton in more recent years. However, the main impetus for specifically philosophical work came with structure, as always.

The first holder of the Chair was Professor Louis Arnaud Reid, who came to philosophy of education after an already distinguished philosophical career. He held the post for 15 years. In 1962, two years before I began my own teaching career, he devoted the whole of his Valedictory Lecture to educational theory and its relationship to philosophy. Louis Arnaud Reid laid the foundations on which Richard Peters and Paul Hirst (the first of the four distinguished contributors to this series), built in the 1960s. Together, they created British analytic philosophy of education in its present form. Their influence and that of colleagues in our Philosophy Department was immense. It had a profound effect in the world of teacher education, both pre-service and in-service, both in this country and throughout the English-speaking world.

From the 1980s, the story changes a little. In common with the other 'foundation' disciplines, philosophy found the going a little tougher. Its special interest in examining the fundamental assumptions on which education and schooling rest did not find enough support in official circles. It was held up in some quarters as an example of the 'barmy theory' which university education departments were allegedly imparting to their students and, in fact, using to lead teachers astray. Too much thinking was seen as dangerous by some people.

Throughout this period, again like its fellow disciplines in education, philosophy of education managed to survive, although in a depleted state. All over Britain, and in fact in many parts of the world, units devoted to its study simply closed down. Chairs were lost and lecturers were asked to teach other areas. So it is with both regret and pride that I have to say that this Institute today is the only place in the country where research and teaching in philosophy of education is still pursued on anything that could be seen as a reasonable scale. Our research community here is strong and vibrant: with staff and research students totalling over 30 people. I want to congratulate my colleagues who have kept it going, who have kept the flame flickering through the lean times as hopefully we move into better times in which the fundamental study of philosophy in education is appreciated.

For the last year or so there have been signs that official circles are actually appreciating the light philosophy can throw on the issues that tantalize us. I am thinking now of the School Curriculum and Assessment Authority (SCAA) Forum on Values, the White Paper's interest in education for citizenship and the current focus of the Qualifications and Curriculum Authority (QCA) on the aims of education and its impending review of the National Curriculum – a timely review which gives a wonderful opportunity for people actually to think fundamentally about what knowledge and skills we want to use the precious time of school to impart.[1] So let us hope that this renewed interest will be matched by renewed resources so that the rhetoric becomes reality.

This series of four lectures celebrates the continued vitality of philosophy of education at the end of its first half century and it looks forward to the contributions that we can expect in the future.

Editor's Note

[1] The references are to:

- the National Forum for Values in Education and the Community, set up by SCAA in 1996; this led to guidance on spiritual, moral, social and cultural development in schools which is being piloted by the successor body to SCAA, the QCA;
- *Excellence in Schools,* a White Paper issued by the New Labour government in 1997;
- a consultation on the aims of education conducted by the QCA from late 1997; as this volume is prepared for press, the report from that exercise is still forthcoming;
- the QCA's review of the National Curriculum, intended to lead to legislative changes in the year 2000.

Introduction

Graham Haydon

The lectures published here, which were given at the Institute of Education in the autumn of 1997, were planned chiefly as a celebration of the continuing vitality of philosophy of education, 50 years after the founding of the first Chair in the subject there. They were not intended to give either a comprehensive overview or a critical analysis of the state of the discipline at the present time. The more modest aim was to include four complementary perspectives:

- an historical account of the development of the subject in Britain;
- a view of the relationship between philosophy of education and philosophy in general;
- a consideration of the role of philosophy in educational research;
- one lecture in which philosophy of education would be heard in action discussing a topic of current concern, in order to offset these overviews of the subject.

The four speakers who rose admirably to the occasion were: Paul Hirst (Emeritus Professor of Education of the University of Cambridge and Visiting Professorial Fellow at the Institute), David E. Cooper (Professor of Philosophy at the University of Durham), David Bridges (Professor of Education and Pro-Vice-Chancellor at the University of East Anglia) and Susan Mendus (Professor of Politics at the University of York). (This was the order in which the lectures were given, although in this volume Mendus's chapter is placed third.) In the next four sections of this Introduction, I shall say a little about each of the speakers and their contribution to the series, drawing on the comments made by the colleagues who chaired the sessions (see Acknowledgements, below).

Paul Hirst

Paul Hirst is especially well placed to describe and discuss the evolution of philosophy of education, with particular attention to its early years in Britain. In his chapter, he gives full credit to the roles in that evolution of the first Professor of the subject at the Institute of Education, Louis Arnaud Reid, and of his successor Richard Peters. What he does not do, modestly, is to detail his own role – a deficiency for which this introduction must compensate. Paul Hirst worked for several years at the Institute with Louis Arnaud Reid. After Reid's retirement, he began a collaboration with Richard Peters which was to continue for many years, even after 1965, when Hirst left the Institute staff to become Professor of Education at King's College, London. In the late 1960s and early 1970s Hirst and Peters were, both in their joint work (including *The Logic of Education*, Routledge, 1970) and in their separate contributions, the two leading figures in the creation of British analytic philosophy of education.

One of the most powerful and influential texts in this new movement of ideas was not a book but a single paper: Hirst's 'Liberal education and the nature of knowledge', published in 1965 (in Archambault, R.D. (ed.), *Philosophical Analysis and Education*. London: Routledge). Not only was this for years one of the most discussed papers within the discipline, but also, more than most works of philosophy of education since that time, the ideas in it were taken up and used in curriculum planning in British schools and in the thinking of the schools inspectorate. The paper is still much cited over 30 years later. When Hirst refers to it now, it is to say how misguided he thinks its approach was – for reasons which will become clear to the reader of his contribution in this volume. However, both the admirers and the detractors of the 1965 article can acknowledge the intellectual power of the vision of liberal education which he presented in it.

In the early 1970s London lost Paul Hirst to Cambridge University, where he became a distinguished director of the Department of Education. Throughout his many years at Cambridge, he continued with as much commitment as ever to assist in the further development of philosophy of education – through the Philosophy of Education Society of Great Britain, through publication and through practical involvement in the improvement of teacher education, both in Cambridge and on a national scale.

After retiring from Cambridge, Paul Hirst accepted an invitation to return to the Institute of Education first as Visiting Professor and, more recently, as Visiting Professorial Fellow. Many participants in the philosophy of education research seminars at the Institute have benefited from his incisive comments on papers. He has also recently collaborated with Patricia White in editing for Routledge a four-volume collection of important articles in analytical philosophy of education from across the world.

In his contribution to this volume, Hirst tells in detail the story of the emergence of analytical philosophy of education up to the early 1980s, and takes an overview of the most important developments since that time. As he says of the last two decades: 'with the incorporation of the analytical approach within the wider traditions of Western philosophy in recent years, philosophy of education has, in parallel, been enriched by a widening of both its approach and its interests'. To have reviewed that wider approach and those wider interests in the same detail would have been impossible in the space available. What Hirst in fact does is to give his considered view of the relationship between philosophy and educational practice, and of the nature of education itself, as an initiation into a far wider range of social practices than those academic practices which had been central in his earlier work.

David E. Cooper

David E. Cooper is a philosopher of broad interests. His association with philosophy of education has been a long one, which has included a period teaching at the Institute of Education in the 1970s, and a term of office as Chair of the Philosophy of Education Society in the 1980s. His contributions to the literature of philosophy of education include *Illusions of Equality* (Routledge, 1980), which is a critique of egalitarian ideas in education, and *Authenticity and Learning* (Routledge, 1983), on Nietszche's educational philosophy. The latter book is tied in with another important strand in Cooper's philosophical work, namely his writing on the continental European philosophical tradition, including books on existentialism and on Heidegger. As he draws on these different 'cultures of philosophy', Cooper's chapter becomes in some respects complementary to Hirst's. Much of the philosophical work in the analytical mode which Hirst reviews, Cooper would see as subscribing to the set of presuppositions he calls 'naturalism' (Hirst himself might not agree). Cooper sets in contrast with naturalism the insights of phenomenology, thus illustrating (although not by design) the enriching of philosophy of education to which Hirst himself refers.

Cooper is one of those rare philosophers who can retain the clarity of argument of the analytical tradition while writing about so-called 'continental' philosophy – 'so-called' because his own work has helped to show the artificiality of the divide between continental and analytical philosophy and the need to transcend that division. He has also done important work in aesthetics and in environmental philosophy; and both of these concerns are brought to bear on his thinking about education in his contribution in this volume.

Cooper was invited to address the relationship between philosophy of education and philosophy at large. Reasonably, he finds that brief rather too broad. However, before moving to his narrower 'self-imposed' brief, he raises important questions about the idea that philosophy of education is a branch of applied philosophy, in which philosophy at large is applied to a particular area of concern. Not only does this presuppose a problematic distinction between the philosophy which is applied and what it is applied to, but, more problematically still, it suggests a one-way relationship, as though it is both necessary and possible first to sort out one's philosophical ideas and only then apply them. The rest of Cooper's chapter exemplifies a more adequate conception of the relationship between philosophy at large and the philosophy of education, in which these activities have to be understood within the context of the wider climate of ideas in which they are carried on.

One interesting point among many in Cooper's chapter is his focus on philosophies of education. During much of the period which Hirst reviews in his chapter, philosophers of education saw themselves as 'doing' the subject, but not as propounding a philosophy of education. Yet, as Cooper points out, it seems clear now that Peters did have a philosophy of education. Probably it could be said that Hirst had a philosophy of (liberal) education in the 1960s and 1970s, and that he now has a different philosophy of education – in which 'education for a good life is not primarily education into theoretical academic disciplines but initiation into social practices in which we can individually find a fulfilling life'. Certainly Hirst and Cooper, who might disagree on many things, seem to agree that philosophy of education cannot be carried on as a self-contained analysis of concepts, independent of other forms of enquiry both within and beyond the broad field of philosophy.

Susan Mendus

A lecture series marking 50 years of philosophy of education would have been unbalanced if it had consisted entirely of reflection on the subject, without showing in depth how the subject can illuminate specific areas of educational concern. One area which has particularly attracted public attention in recent years is that of moral education. This is also one of the longest standing concerns of philosophical reflection on education, going back to Plato and Aristotle; and what also goes back to Plato and Aristotle is that reflection on moral education cannot be separated from political concerns. Moral education or socialization in some form is inescapable in any society; many philosophers have considered that what form it can and should take turns on the nature of the society in question.

Hirst in his chapter refers to the enormously influential work of certain philosophers in the 1970s and 1980s, including Rawls, Rorty, MacIntyre and Taylor. All of these – and others outside North America, such as Raz and Habermas – have contributed to an ongoing and lively discussion within moral and political philosophy in which the presuppositions of liberalism are being variously reaffirmed or rejected, and much consideration is being given to questions of diversity and of community. In this area, it is easy to see the inappropriateness of the one-way model of the application of philosophy to education which Cooper criticizes; consideration of how far individuals should be – or inescapably must be – brought up within particular moral traditions goes to the heart of the debates between liberals and communitarians. It is no accident, then, that many philosophers of education have been engaging in these same debates, and that much recent philosophical writing on moral education has been asking what kind of moral education is possible and desirable in a society which is, or aspires to be, liberal, democratic and plural.

Susan Mendus, who takes up this theme, began her academic career as a lecturer in philosophy and Morrell Fellow in Toleration in the Department of Politics in the University of York. Her early work was on toleration, its meaning, its scope and its limits. In her book *Toleration and the Limits of Liberalism* (Macmillan, 1989), and in her work since then, she has subjected to questioning the salience of the notion of autonomy in liberal thinking, asking whether liberalism puts too much emphasis on self-direction at the expense of concern for others.

These writings alone are rich in educational implications, but in addition Susan Mendus has published a number of papers directly on educational matters, including education in a multicultural society and the nature of higher education in conditions of modernity. Often in these papers, she has sought to find a middle way between seemingly opposed sets of considerations. Her contribution to this volume is characteristic in this respect. She argues that in modern democratic societies the teaching of moral values appears both imperative and impossible. The route she tries to negotiate through this impasse requires the educator to offer two things, namely an awareness of the intransigent nature of moral conflict in conditions of modernity, and a recognition that this intransigence does not remove the moral responsibility of the individual. Thus, the controversial but stimulating conclusion is that the emphasis is to be put not where others may want to put it, that is on the possibility of common values, but on the inescapability of individual responsibility.

David Bridges

The chapter by David Bridges provides a fitting conclusion to this volume. Not only does it offer a very personal perspective on some of the same developments which Hirst addresses, but it also takes up an important matter which was left open in Hirst's account. For Hirst, 'it is absurd to seek to develop educational practices whilst ignoring all that can be known in the strict theoretical disciplines of educational studies. Philosophy of education is ... precisely one of those theoretical disciplines'. However, there are other disciplines too, and Hirst's chapter says nothing about the relationship between philosophical and other disciplines of educational studies. This is the issue Bridges takes up, and, in the process, he offers something like a programme for the future of philosophy of education.

David Bridges is Professor of Education and Pro-Vice-Chancellor at the University of East Anglia. In the first section of his chapter, he fills in the early history of his own engagement with philosophy and with education. Along the way, he reveals something of how the teaching of philosophy of education has changed, as conceptions of its nature have changed. I cannot imagine that the first essay question put to students of the subject at the Institute of Education now would be 'Are synthetic *a priori* truths possible?'.

For many years, from 1968, Bridges taught at Homerton College, Cambridge. He was Deputy Principal there before leaving for East Anglia in 1990. By then, he had also produced a steady stream of philosophical publications on a wide range of educational topics, including democracy and education, discussion in education, mixed ability teaching and accountability. Throughout that period and subsequently, he has also had a substantial involvement in educational research and evaluation. In recent years, he has drawn this involvement in research and philosophy together by exploring the interface between the two. In doing this, he has constantly argued, both at the Conferences of the Philosophy of Education Society of Great Britain and the Conferences of the British Educational Research Association, that philosophers and educational researchers should be working much more closely together.

To a considerable extent, as Bridges details, the world of educational research has either been ignorant of, or has simply ignored, the contribution that philosophy can make. However, it is not enough, of course, for philosophers of education simply to point this out. They have to demonstrate the value of their contribution, and do this in a climate in which educational research in general is not highly regarded by politicians or by many educational practitioners. How, then, can the relationship between philosophy of education and educational research be reconstructed in a way that will be of benefit, not only to these areas themselves, but (most importantly) to educational practice? Bridges sets out his own answer to this question.

As the answer given is Bridges' own, I want to digress to explain why this volume does not take up the suggestion (from an anonymous reader) that it should end with 'a short conclusion from the point of view of the Institute of Education, responding to the range of issues raised and indicating how the [lectures] and the publication might inform further work at the Institute.'

First, although there are many references to the Institute of Education in this volume – reflecting the important role that the Institute has played in the development of philosophy of education in Britain – the chapters were never intended to be specifically about the progress and prospects of the subject at the Institute. The subject itself was central to the lectures, and it was in this spirit that they were jointly sponsored by the Institute and by the Philosophy of Education Society of Great Britain. The Society too has played an important part in the development of the subject, through its conferences and through *The Journal of Philosophy of Education*, and if the contributors to this volume have all, in varying degrees, had links with the Institute, they have also all been active in the Society.

Second, what would be a conclusion 'from the point of view of the Institute of Education'? Although I work at the Institute and am a member of the Society, the present remarks are mine, not those of the Institute or of the Society. In his opening remarks (now the Preface of this volume), the current Director of the Institute, Peter Mortimore, has spoken very positively of the contribution that philosophy of education can make, given the resources. However, an official Institute point of view presumably would have to be a statement drafted and redrafted as it passed through various committees – by which time it would hardly make for lively reading. In a similar way, the Society does not have a position on the relationship between philosophy and educational research. It is arguable that it should, but at the time of writing it does not, and it is not to be expected that all members individually would agree on anything that went beyond the bland.

David Bridges' proposals, then, stand – not with official authority behind them, but with the authority of his own long experience and engagement in philosophy, education and educational research – as a challenge to both philosophers of education and educational researchers, as that term is conventionally understood.

Acknowledgements

As editor of this volume I have benefited from the comments of an anonymous reader. If these have taken the published version somewhat further from what the audience at the lectures actually heard, they have improved it as a book.

I would like to acknowledge especially the contribution made to the success of the series by the distinguished academic colleagues who chaired the lectures. In the order in which the chapters are printed here, they are: John White, who holds not the established Chair (which has been unfilled since the retirement of Richard Peters), but a personal Chair in philosophy of education at the Institute; Richard Norman, Professor of Philosophy at the University of Kent at Canterbury; Terry McLaughlin, University Lecturer in Education at the University of Cambridge and Secretary of the Philosophy of Education Society at the time of the lectures; and Wilfred Carr, Professor of Education at the University of Sheffield and Chair of the Society. Their prepared introductions and their impromptu replies to the lectures helped to put the lectures in context for the audience and to raise questions for further thought. Spoken remarks on such occasions do not always transfer well to the printed page. The Chairpersons have endured patiently both my attempts to recast their remarks and the eventual decision to replace four separate introductions by this single introduction, in which I have drawn on their ideas and sometimes their own words.

Finally, I would like to express my own thanks, and those of my colleagues in Philosophy of Education at the Institute, to Peter Mortimore for introducing the series, and to both co-sponsors for their support and financial help, without which the series could not have been mounted.

Graham Haydon
Institute of Education
July 1998

1 Philosophy of Education: The Evolution of a Discipline

Paul H. Hirst

Louis Arnaud Reid

When in 1947 Louis Arnaud Reid took office as Professor of Philosophy of Education at the Institute of Education, London, the university world and the world of educational studies in general was for the first time in Britain, and indeed arguably in the world, giving public expression and recognition to the importance of the sustained, coherent and systematic philosophical study of educational beliefs and practices. What was not recognized we can be sure was that the occasion was inaugurating the development of philosophy of education as a distinct area of academic philosophy and as a discipline central to educational theory and practice in the exciting way in which that was to occur. Indeed, more was going to be needed than the circumstances of 1947 could provide for the establishment of this new discipline. Still the then Director of the Institute, Dr G.B. Jeffrey, had the vision and the initiative to make the first breakthrough.

Of course, he was not acting without clear leads from within the history of educational ideas and the steady evolution of educational study. Indeed, philosophers since the pre-Socratics, including some of the most important, had contributed significantly to the development of Western educational thought and practice. However, in most cases they had done this incidentally to their more fundamental and more sophisticated work in epistemology, ethics or social philosophy. There had been little sense that their ideas on education might constitute a developing and increasingly sophisticated tradition, progressively illuminating the nature and significance of education. At best, there had seemed to be merely a series of distinct and alternative points of view on education propounded by philosophically minded individuals. However, the progressive development in the twentieth century of more specialized studies of education, in the history of education, educational psychology and the sociology of education, began to throw up repeatedly the inescapable importance of philosophical beliefs about the nature of human beings, the nature and foundations of knowledge, the nature of morality for educational aims and practices, and the need for these to be more systematically examined.

Only in the United States had any direct link between sophisticated contemporary academic philosophy and educational practice previously emerged when John Dewey, a prominent pragmatist, became directly involved in the development of experimental schooling inspired by the substantive epistemological, ethical and political philosophy for which he argued. Here, for the first time was something worthy of being called philosophy of education, a study directed at current educational issues, albeit from a very specific and radically controversial philosophical position. Dewey's personal influence on educational thought and practice was very considerable in the United States and in due course led to the establishment of a tradition of philosophy of education based on his ideas. However, for many diverse reasons, institutional, sociological and political as well as philosophical, the serious study of education with more wide-ranging philosophical links than his particular pragmatic theories failed to emerge for a considerable period.

Long before Dr Jeffrey, successive Directors at the Institute of Education, London had shown a deep awareness of and interest in the philosophical aspects of educational questions. The first Director, Sir Percy Nunn, wrote a quite strongly philosophical book, *Education: Its*

Data and First Principles, as early as 1920. His successor, Sir Fred Clarke, took on lecturing on 'The Principles of Education' in a way that reflected his wide-ranging interests in philosophical as well as sociological questions and it was he who first pressed for the appointment of specialist lecturers in these distinct areas. However, it was his successor, Dr Jeffrey, who specifically proposed that, in the major post-war development of the Institute, there should be Chairs established in Philosophy of Education and Sociology of Education, alongside those already existing within the University in Educational Psychology, History of Education and Comparative Education. Jeffrey, previously a distinguished Professor of Mathematics, with a strong commitment to the importance of the academic study of education and considerable personal interest in philosophy, had a clear view of what was needed for the development of philosophy of education. Above all he held there must be a Chair in the subject, occupied by a top-level, internationally recognised, academic philosopher working within the central traditions of the subject, who, using his knowledge and expertise, would focus on educational issues and introduce student teachers and experienced teachers to the philosophical aspects of their work. Louis Arnaud Reid fitted the bill admirably. Already a Professor of Philosophy of considerable distinction and with wide interests, he had published significantly in ethics, philosophy of religion and aesthetics. The only question was whether someone of his standing would take on this difficult, quite new and open-ended job. He took some persuading but once committed he set about things with considerable determination.

At that time (1947) the world of academic philosophy in Britain was in a fairly chaotic state. In the pre-war period, the development of what came to be known as 'analytical philosophy' and the iconoclastic ideas of 'logical positivism', notably voiced in A.J. Ayer's *Language, Truth and Logic* (1936), produced much dispute and discussion but the war intervened before these ideas even began to be adequately digested. During the war, a nucleus of philosophers pursued some of these ideas further, notably in Cambridge, where Ludwig Wittgenstein held court with a select group of followers, but it was only in the post-war context that this new and challenging work could be faced directly and its significance explored. Much of it was difficult, detailed and very technical in character, being concerned with such fundamental matters as the nature of meaning and truth, and the character of language and logic. What the significance of these new ideas might be for educational thought was something no-one could begin to envisage at that time.

For Professor Reid there were much more immediate tasks for him to engage in. From an already well-developed philosophical position, he set about introducing students and staff at the Institute to sustained philosophical questioning and reasoning about educational aims and values and the activities of teaching. He insisted that educators get inside philosophical thinking rather than simply study the history of educational ideas from Plato to Whitehead. In lectures he philosophized in front of his students and demanded that there be follow-ups in small discussion seminars. In substantive terms, he argued with great insight and sensitivity for a distinctive approach to the relationships between knowledge, experience, feeling, intuition and action, and from these he sought to characterize the modes of experience and understanding that constitute human life. On the basis of delineating the central features of moral, personal, aesthetic, religious and scientific understanding, he then tried to set out the fundamental issues in education. In his constant search for clarity and the justification of claims, his approach was exploratory. To some, especially students wanting ready answers to the pressing problems encountered on teaching practice in schools, his lecturing was frustrating and lacking in force. He was at times himself equally frustrated by the difficulties of getting students, totally unused to philosophical questions, to appreciate the importance of such considerations when so little time was available. However, he persisted and achieved much of real importance. He exemplified philosophy of education as a living practice, that of the sustained, systematic philosophical examination of educational issues. He clearly mapped certain major areas in which philosophy of education must operate, notably the content of education and the character of its domains, the significance and nature of the value judgements that educational practices involve, and the importance in this area of the fundamental issues of freedom and discipline. In fact, he launched philosophy of education as an academic discipline, breaking the firm and somewhat restrictive hold on educational study which the other disciplines in that field had so far established.

Throughout his time at the Institute, Professor Reid was well aware of the changes taking place in academic philosophy. He was much concerned that advanced students, staff and interested school teachers, particularly those with some philosophical background, should be able to listen to and discuss with prominent philosophers of the day. To this end, he established the annual Easter School of Philosophy as a residential vacation course. Nevertheless, he found much that was then being developed, under the label of 'analytical philosophy', thoroughly uncongenial. He regretted what he saw as an obsession with analysis. He thought the epistemological basis of much of it was too concerned with propositional rather than other kinds of knowledge and too devoted to scientific paradigms. Against this, he sharpened his own philosophical position and defended it with great care and integrity. He was very much a man of his times and had great qualities, academic and personal, that did much to establish at the Institute of Education a climate in which philosophy of education could take root. When Richard Peters succeeded him in the Chair in 1962, all was set academically and institutionally for the discipline to develop apace and it did so in quite a remarkable fashion.

The Twentieth-century Philosophical Background

To begin to understand what happened it is necessary, I think, to glance back to changes in academic philosophy that first emerged in the early twentieth century. In the early 1900s, reviving the long-established empiricist tradition stemming from the work of Locke, Berkeley and Hume, two Cambridge philosophers, G.E. Moore and Bertrand Russell, asserted, although with very different emphases, the central importance of 'analysis' as a philosophical method. By this they meant the elucidation of the meaning of any concept, idea or unit of thought used when seeking to understand ourselves and our world, by reducing it and breaking it down into more basic concepts that constitute it, and thereby showing its relationship to a network of other concepts or discovering what the concept denotes. By such conceptual analysis, they sought to clarify the meaning of beliefs in order more readily to establish their justification and truth. To Russell this was an endeavour to establish the foundations of all valid knowledge claims in sense experience. Moore was concerned with the grounding of knowledge in basic simple intuitive common-sense claims into which more complex concepts and beliefs could be broken down in analysis. For both, and the younger philosopher Wittgenstein who joined them in Cambridge, the relationship between language and reality, or words and the world, became a crucial issue. It was claimed by Russell and Wittgenstein that to adequately do its job in the development of knowledge, language must be stripped of all vagueness of meaning so as to convey sharply determined concepts and propositions that are necessarily either true or false in empirical terms. Clear meaning must be built in a language that pictures in basic atomic elements states of affairs which can be directly discerned in sense experience. It is by the logical-linguistic analysis of assertive propositional sentences that we can reductively establish their meaning and truth or falsity. By such analysis, major problems in metaphysics and epistemology were claimed to be nothing more than confusions in the language being used, many traditional philosophical beliefs thereby being characterized as quite literally meaningless.

Wittgenstein's ideas as set out in his *Tractatus Logico-Philosophicus* (1922) had a profound influence on a limited group of philosophers, particularly members of the famed Vienna Circle, several of whom asserted that to know the meaning of any proposition is, through analysis, to come to know the method of its verification or its empirical truth conditions. To other philosophers, the more wide-ranging and generous notion of analysis pursued by Moore was more suited to the richness of human understanding than Wittgenstein's and Russell's restrictive and technical approach. What was more, the attempt to develop in detail this technical programme proved to be fraught with ever expanding difficulties so that its whole account of the relationship of words to the world, and hence of meaning, came into question. That what can be meaningfully expressed is necessarily capable of being set out in language that ultimately pictures or mirrors in propositional form the structure of the world began to give way to a radically different view, that language can meaningfully take on many different forms devised according to diverse human interests and purposes, constrained only by our naturally given abilities and the context of our lives.

In the 1930s, Wittgenstein himself came to totally reject the whole approach to meaning and the reductive account of analysis that he had propounded in the *Tractatus*. What came to replace it was the recognition that the meaning of concepts, propositions and all other forms of discourse is to be found in the uses for which language is employed. It is in the rules that govern the use of terms, the conditions and criteria for their application and their links to shared public activities and events, that we can grasp their meaning. In these terms analysis is concerned to map out how our language operates in communicating meaning by setting out how concepts are related to each other, no matter how complex that might be, and how meaning functions in our many diverse 'forms of life', for example, in our understanding of the physical world, expressing emotions, making promises, praying, playing games, issuing orders or teaching. Analysis so understood asserts no logical propositional form as fundamental to meaning. It asserts no mirroring of the world nor any other one account of the link between words and experience. Propositional meaning is in no way just a matter of truth conditions of an empirical or any other kind. Significant concepts are not presumed to have a central or essential meaning that is determinate because of a strict set of necessary and sufficient conditions for their use. Concepts may be open and overlapping in their criteria of application. All of which means that analysis is not now seen as in any sense a reductive exercise, but as one which explores conceptual connections in our use of language, thus seeking to sort out confusions in the discourse in which our understanding and knowledge are embedded.

In such analyses, Wittgenstein endeavoured to elucidate the misunderstandings that arise when we are bemused by language's superficial structure. We mistakenly take nouns such as 'mind', 'concept' or 'number' to designate entities having at least some of the properties of objects even if abstract and immaterial. We take 'thinking' and 'willing' to be activities like physical activities yet somehow to be totally 'inner', private and independent of what is 'outer' and public, thus being seriously misled in our understanding of persons, their lives and indeed their education. In a similar way, Wittgenstein saw our discourse as infected by deeply distorting analogies. Thus, philosophical problems are above all disorders in our conceptual schemes that analysis can cure. By conceptual analysis, therefore, we can be delivered from mistaken beliefs that confuse our understanding and our conduct. Our conceptual frameworks can be rendered more coherent, thereby enabling the development of more rational beliefs and practices.

Although Wittgenstein developed his later ideas whilst in Cambridge between 1929 and 1947, the major revolution in philosophy which he caused largely took shape in Oxford during the post-war period through the influence of his students who increasingly worked there and through notes of his lectures and classes circulated widely prior to the publication of his epoch-making book, *Philosophical Investigations*, in 1953. By 1960, important analytical work had been done on major traditional philosophical problems such as that by Ryle (1949) on the nature of mind and Cartesian dualism, Austin (1962) on the concepts of perception and truth, and Strawson (1959) on some of the most general metaphysical categories that underpin our understanding. Others worked at less fundamental levels for instance on responsibility and punishment in law (Hart, 1968), on the language of morals (Hare, 1952) and the nature of historical explanation (Gardiner, 1952). However, it would be a mistake to think that these and other philosophers fully accepted Wittgenstein's later views of philosophy or analysis and its techniques. Certain approaches and particular forms of argument used in earlier stages of the development of analysis were not infrequently held to be useful even if their original significance was no longer accepted. Opinions were divided on such issues as the status of ordinary language in Wittgenstein's work, on his seeming radical linguistic relativism, on the notion of paradigm cases of conceptual use, on the precise relationship between meaning and verification, and on Wittgenstein's espousing some form of philosophical, if not scientific, behaviourism. Yet his influence was very far reaching. Soon no traditional view of philosophy was untouched and the impetus to employ analytical methods in new areas of theoretical and practical debate was considerable.

It was in this richly developing philosophical context that certain philosophers in the early 1960s first really began systematically to analyse the central concepts in which our major educational beliefs are commonly constructed. How analytical work might be pursued in the area had been most tellingly heralded in Ryle's *Concept of Mind* as early as 1949, with its extended discussion of such educationally important concepts as those of knowledge, skills, intelligence and dispositions, and in Hare's direct concern for the character of moral education in his book *The Language of Morals* (1952). However, in 1958 Israel Scheffler, an academic philosopher at Harvard University also working in education and who was increasingly influenced by analytical developments, edited a collection of forward-looking papers, *Philosophy of Education* (1958). He followed this in 1960 with his more important book, *The Language of Education*, in which he sought to analyse the character and use of different categories of educational discourse and to map the central conceptual features within our concepts of teaching.

Richard Peters

It was at this very time that Richard Peters turned to the analysis of educational concepts and spent a period on sabbatical leave at Harvard with Israel Scheffler. Peters was already well known for his analytical work on the concept of motivation (1958) and his publications in social and political theory. He was soon tipped as the ideal person to succeed Professor Reid and to the delight of everyone concerned with the appointment, in due time he moved to the Institute of Education. He very quickly became a dominant figure in the Institute, academically and personally, provoking enormous interest in philosophy of education through major lectures, his inaugural lecture *Education as Initiation* (1964) and his highly influential major book *Ethics and Education* (1966). In these, he embarked on a detailed analysis of the concept of education itself and the fundamental ethical and social principles on which the content and conduct of education could be coherently and rationally based.

So what were the distinguishing features of the subject as it grew under Peters' leadership? These are perhaps most clearly set out in his first paper that stated his own view of the matter, and in the Introduction to *Ethics and Education*. In these he outlined the 'second order' concern of philosophy with forms of thought and argument expressed in Socrates' questions, 'What do you mean?' and 'How do you know?', and in Kant's questions about what is presupposed by our forms of thought and awareness. In his own words, he maintained that the philosopher is engaged in 'the disciplined demarcation of concepts, the patient explication of the grounds of knowledge and presuppositions of different forms of discourse' (Peters, 1996: 15).

> Philosophers make explicit the conceptual schemes which (competing) beliefs and standards presuppose: they examine their consistency and search for criteria for their justification. This does not imply that philosophers can only produce an abstract rationale of what is in existence, like a high-level projection of the plan of a house. For enquiry at this level can develop with some degree of autonomy. Presuppositions can be drastically criticized and revised; grounds for belief can be challenged and new ones suggested; conceptual schemes can be shown to be radically inconsistent or inapplicable; new categorizations can be constructed.
>
> (Peters, 1966: 16)

Peters (1966) suggests four main areas of work:

- the analysis of concepts specific to education, an area which can be seen as falling under philosophical psychology and social philosophy;
- the application of ethics and social philosophy to assumptions about the desirable content and procedures of education;
- an examination of the conceptual schemes and assumptions used by educational psychologists about educational processes;
- an examination of the philosophical character of the content and organization of the curriculum and related questions about learning.

In this characterization of philosophy of education, it is important to note that from the start Peters refused to be dogmatic about the nature of philosophical analysis. This openness was no doubt in part the result of his very considerable studies in classical philosophy, the history of modern philosophy – especially social philosophy and the British empiricists – and the history of psychology. It is no doubt also in part the result of the many different contemporary influences on him during his formative years, influences ranging from the work of Moore, Ryle and Wittgenstein to the personal impact of study and collaboration with Popper, A.C. Mace, Oakeshott, Hamlyn and Phillips Griffiths.

Thus, the central features of Peters' philosophical position were being formed when new and distinctive types of philosophical analysis were being developed and hotly disputed. At times, he voiced his own uncertainties about the character of techniques and the precise significance of their results. This can be seen in his return from time to time to a number of topics of central concern to him, especially the analysis of the concept of education and the justification of the content of education. At times, he clearly used forms of argument that suggested that some 'central' or 'essential' meaning of a concept, such as 'education', might be elucidated as an anchor for future deliberations and that perhaps universally. Yet he was aware that if this analysis was to be taken as setting out what education should entail in practice then its practical adoption would need the most rigorous justification. He became more and more sceptical about any search for universal notions, recognizing increasingly the influence of the social context on all conceptual schemes. He also later recognized how few concepts of significance in education, or elsewhere, can be sharply analysed in terms of clear necessary and sufficient conditions for their use.

He was likewise never concerned dogmatically to defend ordinary language as if it provided Moorean-type foundations for meaning or knowledge. Indeed, he was much concerned about the development of the specialist understanding available to educationists in psychology and sociology and the importance of philosophers working in constant association with such specialists in the development of educational theory. Further, he considered it necessary for there to be, and he himself sought to provide, arguments setting out the place of the conceptual schemes of common sense within psychological research. What he sought to do in education was to examine the language educationists use, whether everyday or technical, so as to explore the concepts underlying this for their coherence and applicability, and thus their significance in educational argument. However, he was also acutely aware that the conceptual apparatus by means of which we understand education is closely interlocked with both the most general conceptual schemes we use and the substantive beliefs we hold concerning the nature of human beings, reason, knowledge, morality and social and political matters. He considered it essential, therefore, that philosophers of education should seek to illuminate the most wide-ranging philosophical context within which educational notions are of their nature to be understood.

Peters set out the task and character of philosophy of education with remarkable perceptiveness. He managed to capture its distinctive features both as a developing domain of contemporary philosophy and as a major discrete area within educational studies. He saw philosophy as a developing discipline, incorporating the methods and achievements of conceptual analysis into its traditional major concerns. He also saw clearly how the discipline could embrace specifically educational issues and thereby contribute profoundly to our understanding of the purposes, content and processes of education.

It was fortuitous that Peters undertook this work as the Institute's involvement in initial and in-service teacher education expanded hugely, especially with the introduction in colleges of education of three-year courses of initial training and then four-year courses for a B.Ed degree. Central to these changes was the demand for much more academically rigorous study of education as crucial to any truly professional training and this was understood as study within the major academic disciplines of educational theory. Thus, there developed a considerable need for colleges to have staff well qualified in these disciplines, by new staff being appointed and existing staff undertaking advanced study. Peters' clear vision of what was required of the Institute of Education in these terms, his personal devotion to the job and the excitement of all this new work attracted an expanding group of philosophically trained school teachers and lecturers to join in the enterprise. The philosophy of education department grew steadily from three faculty members to ten who shared to a considerable degree Peters' interests and aspirations, whilst complementing each other in their educational and philosophical expertise. By 1980, a considerable body of significant work had been published in the subject, primarily by those at the Institute of Education or closely linked with it. With a steady stream of advanced students from home and overseas, a flourishing academic journal and The Philosophy of Education Society of Great Britain run successfully for over 15 years, the discipline could by then claim to be firmly established in academic and institutional terms both within Britain and indeed throughout the English-speaking world.

Developments outside Britain

In the United States the early development of analytical philosophy of education was altogether more restrained than in Britain, taking place against a very different background in academic philosophy and in different institutional circumstances. Until well into the twentieth century, US philosophy was dominated by the indigenous pragmatism of Pierce, James and Dewey with its strong scientific roots. Therefore, it is not surprising that when analytical philosophy began to have some impact there during the 1930s it was the early analytical ideas of members of the Vienna Circle, several of whom moved to the United States, that were most influential. The strong empiricism and deep interest in the philosophy of science that resulted had, and continues even now to have, a profound effect on US philosophy.

By the mid 1950s, when the later analytical approach of Wittgenstein was transforming British philosophy, the greatest force on the US scene was the work of Quine (1953), who although sharing something of Wittgenstein's later ideas nevertheless radically rejected the most fundamental tenets of his approach. Quine was a convinced empiricist seeing all meaning and knowledge as scientific in character, even philosophical understanding. Meaning, he held, is rooted in a behaviourist account of language in which words are related to the world causally. For Wittgenstein, by contrast, the relationship is a matter of conventional rules which can be broken or changed. As a result, meaning is not to be equated with any system of behavioural responses to words but in the conventionally established rules for the uses to which we put words. However complex in detail, Quine's view of meaning and knowledge is still in the end a form of empirical reductionism. To Wittgenstein, meaning is to be found in the very diverse language games we have devised in which we make sense of ourselves and our world.

It was against Quine's distinctly antipathetic major influence in academic philosophy and the existence of a variety of other rival approaches, traditional and contemporary such as Neo-Thomism and Existentialism, that analytical philosophy in Wittgenstein's later sense had to make its way. However, it did so with steady progress, mainly in the hands of Americans who had spent time in Oxford. From 1960, analytical philosophy of education equally began to grow steadily in a number of different centres, notably Harvard, Teachers' College Columbia and Illinois, although without either the major grouping or the institutional support found in London. However, through the medium of the Philosophy of Education Society and the journals *Educational Theory* and *Studies in Philosophy and Education*, the analytical tradition took root in the United States, largely independent of any connections with the Institute of Education, London.

In Australasia and Canada work was initiated primarily by university teachers strongly influenced by work in London, who were joined by others who had studied in the United States, notably in Illinois. In Sydney the influence of John Anderson, a senior Australian academic philosopher with a long-standing interest in educational questions, combined with the influence of Quine's ideas to give a distinctive controversial focus and radical stamp to some of the work there. Throughout Australasia, the links with London grew slowly weaker and the subject developed its own ethos and agenda with a flourishing Philosophy of Education Society and a major international journal, *Educational Philosophy and Theory*.

After 1980

By 1980 Philosophy of Education was a robust discipline with its own momentum, constantly drawing life and energy from developments in academic philosophy and from demands for ever more rationally constructed educational theory and practice. Its achievement over some 20 years had been remarkable. It included, appropriately, self-conscious analysis of the subject's own philosophical character and its place within the wide field of educational theory as a whole. The very nature of education had been analytically mapped out and examined as never before, as had its purposes and their justification. The conceptual structure of beliefs about the nature of human beings and their capacities and the place of such considerations in education had been exposed with greater clarity. The social and philosophical significance of education had been located within the context of fundamental social concepts and principles. Many of the central concepts and beliefs in terms of which we determine and structure the content and practices of education had been analysed and critically examined. Yet in all these areas the work done served only to reveal what more was waiting to be tackled. Here was but the start of an enterprise in our understanding of education in which analysis would have wider and more detailed application and in which its approach would receive the critical self-reflection required of any sophisticated discipline.

However, by the early 1980s, there were already indications that analytical philosophy in general was changing its character in significant respects. Conceptual analysis as exemplified in Wittgenstein's *Philosophical Investigations* was no longer being seen as philosophy's only concern. It became widely held that such work resulted not only in the removal of confusions in the conceptual schemes of our common discourse, but in strong if tacit support for our most fundamental beliefs within those schemes, concerning, for instance, the nature of persons, language, knowledge, society and moral values. As it became clear that different social groups of religious believers, political theorists, moral philosophers, epistemologists and educationalists manifestly use alternative conceptual schemes, some saw conceptual relativism as the only possible outcome of analysis. Others saw Wittgenstein's notion of 'forms of life', which our conceptual schemes articulate, as indicating that sustained analysis itself ultimately must lead to an anchorage of understanding that is by no means entirely relative but rooted in given features of human life and its context. In the 1980s long-standing traditional philosophical beliefs were coming fully to the fore, their validity now being examined analytically and critically in relation to their social and historical contexts. Analytical work was leading to a new consideration of issues well established in the whole history of philosophy. Indeed, reconnected with its own historical roots analytical philosophy was itself becoming part of the long tradition of philosophy and a powerful revitalizing force within it.

The transformation that was to take place throughout academic philosophy at the time was heralded above all in social and political philosophy by Rawls' outstanding book *A Theory of Justice* (1972). Rorty's *Philosophy and the Mirror of Nature* (1980) inaugurated a massive reconsideration of the foundations of knowledge. At the same time, MacIntyre's *After Virtue* (1981) had a similar impact on moral philosophy and Charles Taylor's papers on human nature and the human sciences (1985) deeply influenced ideas about persons and their social relations. In the 1980s, the centre of this wide-ranging work progressively moved from Oxford to a number of universities in the United States, promoted significantly by a much increased transatlantic exchange and institutional changes in British universities which encouraged certain prominent philosophers to move to the United States. Yet in philosophy (as in most other areas) the academic community was becoming increasingly unified internationally, embracing new interests and emphases. By the late 1990s, work with strong roots in the analytical tradition has considerable involvement with work from other traditions, notably those of neo-Marxism and critical theory, existentialism and postmodernism. Still there can no doubt of the continuing importance and achievements of the analytical tradition developed over nearly a century.

Against this background, analytical philosophy of education since 1980 has above all been marked by much re-assessment and re-working of the most fundamental issues within the discipline. This subject has paralleled and, of course, highly benefited from the fundamental work that has been undertaken in all the major branches of academic philosophy on which philosophy of education must draw. Recent work has been notable for its much wider philosophical interests and scope and its much greater detail. Earlier work can now be seen to have presupposed without adequate critical examination many philosophical beliefs and forms of argument associated with the Enlightenment and particularly Kant. The widely held conceptual framework that was elucidated with care and subtlety in the early years of the discipline is now widely understood as justifying a particular view of the relationship between theory and practice and a particular conception of the educated person as a rationally autonomous individual. Approaches to moral and social education, educational content and its structure, teaching, motivation and many other features of education were mapped and defended in much detail within this scheme. However, once its underlying concepts (such as those of the individual person, society, right, good and reason) were seriously challenged within academic philosophy, a wide ranging debate on the general character of education and on detailed understanding of it was inevitably opened up. Much of great importance has been, and is still being, learnt in the debates within the discipline. Not that the earlier understanding of education is simply rejected. Far from it. Much of the conceptual mapping and many of the arguments retain their validity if their place on our over-all understanding of education is not now as it was previously held to be. The relationship of the individual to society is currently being elucidated as never before, as is the constitutive nature of persons, too. What constitutes human flourishing and the formation and conduct of good lives is being formulated anew. The implications of this work for our grasp of what education entails, not only in its most general terms, but also in more specific details, are clearly considerable.

The Nature of Education and of Philosophy of Education

It is my personal view that philosophy of education is now steadily elucidating a new and more adequate characterization of education that is closely related to significant developments in academic philosophy.

Those developments concern primarily our understanding of human nature, the relationship of individuals in society and the place of reason in human life. In the 1960s and 1970s, under the spell of the rationalist climate of the time, education was seen as providing the foundations of a good life by promoting the development of a rationally autonomous individual. This was held to require initiation into the achievements of reason in knowledge and understanding in the sciences, social sciences, humanities, arts and religion and the personal application of such knowledge in the individual's context. Such a view is based on seeing the exercise of reason as necessarily the use of our cognitive powers, independent of all other capacities, to achieve propositional knowledge and understanding to which all other aspects of life must then conform. However, contemporary philosophical work has radically challenged such a view of the operation of reason in the living of a rational life. Thus, it has challenged the idea of education as centrally the acquisition of propositional, or abstracted, detached theoretical knowledge and understanding.

There are I would argue the strongest grounds for judging that reason operates most fundamentally in the satisfaction of physical, psychological and social needs and interests and that, in so doing, it operates in a form distinct from its operation in developing propositional or theoretical understanding and knowledge. What it is rational to do in the satisfaction of needs and interests is discovered directly in activity itself, in the trial and error of experiment. What is rational is what is successful in experience. Having a reason for an action is, thus, the product of practical experience in which we discover and develop both our needs and their satisfactions. In exercising our cognitive capacities in this context, we conceptualize and articulate our needs and interests. We classify objects, events, patterns of behaviour, principles of action, not in abstract 'disinterested' propositional terms, but in discourse that encapsulates our practical experience of the world. We develop practical knowledge in the exercise of practical reason.

As social beings, with interlocking and common needs and interests and common capacities, we develop, in this exercise of practical reason, great webs of social practices developed precisely for the fulfilment of ourselves as human beings. To live a good life is then to find individually a life of fulfilment in relation to rationally developed social practices created experimentally as evolving traditions. Seen in this way, education for a good life is not primarily education into theoretical academic disciplines but initiation into social practices in which we can individually find a fulfilling life.

If education is characterized in these terms, it will be directly concerned above all with those practices needed by all for a good life in our contemporary context. Such practices will concern our management of ourselves in physical terms in our natural and technological environment and our establishing and sustaining personal and social relationships. They will relate to such matters as finance, law, politics and vocational roles. Beyond these, there will be many practices in the arts, religion, sports and other voluntary activities that play a significant part in fulfilling life for many. There are also many practices of theoretical reason in the academic disciplines, but I would maintain these are not themselves essential elements in all individual good lives although they are crucial elements in the rational development of all other social practices as will be indicated below. The central tenet here is that social practices and practical reason are the fundamental concerns of education, not propositional knowledge and theoretical reason.

However, my concern for the importance of practical reason has further consequences for our understanding of education. In keeping with my general thesis, all practices in the conduct of education, from those concerned with organizing an educational system to those of running a school, planning a curriculum, or teaching reading can be rationally developed only in critically reflective experiment in practice itself. Such rational development necessitates the generation of practical discourse and practical theory in which successful practices are expressed and critically examined. Yet such practices and the attendant practical theory involve assumptions about human nature, the nature of reason, the relationship of individuals to society, the nature and structure of emotions and so on. It is, I suggest, the function of academic theoretical disciplines to search out such presuppositions and examine them in a disinterested fashion. Just as it is absurd to engage in experimental development in, say, engineering practice without knowledge of related fundamental sciences, so it is absurd to seek to develop educational practices whilst ignoring all that can be known in the strict theoretical disciplines of educational studies. Philosophy of education is, I suggest, precisely one of those theoretical disciplines and it is in the achievement of the analytical advances in the subject that its significance for educational practices is being more clearly defined. In these terms, philosophy of education is above all the instrument for the elucidation of those conceptual structures in which we seek to make sense of education. It is the mapper of conceptual schemes and the shaper of concepts into more coherent forms. It is the discerner of the forms of logically coherent argument in the exercise of practical as well as theoretical reason in educational matters. It is the examiner of presuppositions in educational thought and practice, especially of those conceptual schemes and patterns of beliefs in which we understand the nature of human beings and what constitutes their good.

Conclusion

I have argued that it was the distinctive, explicit approach of analytical philosophy to the fundamental questions of meaning, justification and presuppositions which provoked the emergence of philosophy of education as a discrete, self-conscious, self-critical academic discipline. That approach was most powerfully deployed in delineating central work for the discipline and in articulating a substantial account of the concerns of education. With the incorporation of the analytical approach within the wider traditions of Western philosophy in recent years, philosophy of education has, in parallel, been enriched by a widening of both its approach and its interests. However, this continuing evolution has only served to accentuate the early characterization and demarcation of the domain which established it as a coherent and developing philosophical pursuit central to educational studies. So understood, the discipline of philosophy of education has, I think, never been in a healthier state academically and those involved in it are currently producing work of the highest distinction and importance. Yet, since the mid 1980s, the institutional support for it has tragically been in serious decline throughout British universities. Public policy in almost all areas of education, including teacher education and research, has been concerned to promote practices based on ideology, often without reference to critical reflection on existing practices, without necessary experimental development and with total disregard for work in the academic disciplines of educational study, indeed frequently with ignorant denigration of those disciplines. In these circumstances, the financing of work within the disciplines has been greatly reduced. It is to be hoped that with recent political changes policies and practices in education will come to be more rationally developed. For that to happen effectively and coherently will require, amongst other things, that universities once more become centres where the disciplines of education flourish and are used to inform experimental developments in policy and practice.

At present, the discipline of philosophy of education thrives largely on its intellectual capital from happier times. The Institute of Education has, under imposed economic and political constraints, had to see the work here shrink from being carried out by 10 philosophers to being run by some 2.5. Those currently involved do an amazing job in the sustaining of the discipline nationally and internationally. Let us hope more enlightened policies for the universities' work in education will soon enable the discipline to contribute again on the scale it should to educational thought and practice. In particular, let us hope that the Institute of Education, which has done more than any other institution worldwide for the formation of philosophy of education, will once again become the flourishing centre for the subject that it surely should be.

References

Austin, J. (1962), *Sense and Sensibilia*. Oxford: Oxford University Press.

Ayer, A.J. (1936), *Language, Truth and Logic*. London: Gollancz.

Gardiner, P. (1952), *The Nature of Historical Explanation*. Oxford: Oxford University Press.

Hacker, P.M.S. (1996), *Wittgenstein's place in 20th Century Analytic Philosophy*. Oxford: Blackwell.

Hare, R.M. (1952), *The Language of Morals*. Oxford: Oxford University Press.

Hart, H.L.A. (1968), *Punishment and Responsibility*. Oxford: Oxford University Press.

MacIntyre, A. (1981), *After Virtue*. London: Duckworth.

Nunn, P. (1920), *Education: Its Data and First Principles*. London: Edward Arnold.

Peters, R.S. (1958), *The Concept of Motivation*. London: Routledge & Kegan Paul.

— (1964), *Education as Initiation* (Inaugural Lecture). London: Evans Bros (Harrups).

— (1966), *Ethics and Education*. London: Allen and Unwin.

Quine, W.V.O. (1953, reprinted in 1966), *From a Logical Point of View*. New York: Harper and Row; Oxford: Blackwell.

Rawls, J. (1972), *A Theory of Justice*. New York and Oxford: Oxford University Press.

Rorty, R. (1980), *Philosophy and the Mirror of Nature*. Oxford: Blackwell.

Ryle, G. (1949), *The Concept of Mind*. London: Hutchinson.

Scheffler, I. (ed.) (1958), *Philosophy of Education*. Boston: Allyn and Bacon.

— (1960), *The Language of Education*. Springfield, Illinois: Charles C. Thomas.

Strawson, P. (1959), *Individuals: An Essay in Descriptive Metaphysics*. London: Methuen.

Taylor, C. (1985), *Philosophical Papers, Vols 1 and 2*. Oxford: Oxford University Press.

Wittgenstein, L. (1922), *Tractatus Logico-Philosophicus*. London: Routledge.

— (1953), *Philosophical Investigations*. Oxford: Blackwell.

2 Educational Philosophies and Cultures of Philosophy

David E. Cooper

Is Philosophy of Education Applied Philosophy?

The brief I was given – politely, of course – was the relation between philosophy of education and philosophy at large. Honoured by the confidence in my ability to say anything useful about this, I nevertheless decided the brief was too wide. Philosophy of education is a motley of diverse activities, and philosophy at large, of course, a much greater one still. So the topic here will be more circumscribed, namely the relation between educational philosophies and cultures of philosophy. Those terms will be explained in due course, and having illustrated that relation with an historical 'case study' suggestive of some general lessons, I will give my view of the recent and contemporary character of the relation.

However, a remark on the wider brief – one which introduces something of a leitmotiv running through the rest of this chapter. It has become almost received wisdom to speak of philosophy of education as an 'applied' branch of philosophy. Richard Peters described it as raising 'no philosophical problems that are *sui generis*', rather as a 'field ... where basic branches of philosophy have application' (Peters, 1966: 18-19). John White reports a near-consensus among today's philosophers of education that 'their discipline is a form of applied philosophy' (White, 1995a: 216).

Taken fairly casually, such comments may be harmless enough. However, the 'application' model can also mislead, be dangerous and shortchange philosophy of education. To begin with, the notion of application involved cannot be either of the serious and relatively precise notions involved when we speak of applied mathematics, or of applying some Californian doctor's theory of nutrition in a dietary regimen. 'Pure' philosophy is not an uninterpreted system whose variables are given an interpretation by philosophers of education; nor is it a theory 'put into practice' by such philosophers. Second, there is uncertainty where to draw the distinction between what is applied and its application. For some, philosophy of education *as such* is applied philosophy, others distinguish between its 'purer', more 'abstract' reaches and its application closer to the chalkface. There is a danger here, namely that as philosophy of education has been classed as a branch of applied philosophy, then unless its contributions have obvious relevance at the chalkface, its practitioners will betray their calling. Thus, we find one author holding that unless 'philosophical ... writing' is in touch with 'current public ... thinking about education', it is 'largely a waste of time' (Winch, 1996: 1). By that criterion, I suggest, the 'philosophical writing' of Plato and Rousseau was 'largely a waste of time'. Moreover, it would drive a wedge between philosophy of education and other allegedly derivative branches of philosophy (such as philosophy of science) whose practitioners are not required always to be addressing obviously 'relevant', 'public' issues.

My greatest worry, however, is that the 'application' model suggests that there is only one-way traffic – *from* 'the basic branches' of philosophy to philosophy of education. There is a long and honourable tradition of philosophers (including Plato, Rousseau, Schiller, Nietzsche and Dewey) for whom reflection on the nature and aims of education is vital to reflection on issues of ethics, epistemology and political philosophy. For example, Plato's educational proposals are often viewed as dictated by political ends which the truly educated person, the philosopher-king, will serve. However, this is to ignore that, for Plato, a criterion of the good state is that it be 'good enough for the philosophic nature' to prosper within it (*Republic*, 1961: 497). Before we can determine whether a state is a good one, we must reflect on what constitutes an educated 'philosophic nature', and see whether the state supports the requisite educational process. Dewey, equally, does not first articulate a political ideal of democracy and then justify a style of education as promoting that ideal. Instead, the pre-eminent merit of a style of political democracy is that it promotes a maximally educative environment. In its encouragement of 'freer interaction between social groups' and other means for fostering 'shared experience', the good state is the good school writ large (Dewey, 1946: 86).

There will be further examples of two-way traffic – that is how reflections on what education is or should be shape wider conceptions of society and the Good, as well as vice-versa. One contemporary philosopher of education writes of 'restoring' to philosophy of education 'some of its lost dignity' (Siegel, 1990: 4). Recognition of reciprocity between it and allegedly more 'basic branches' is surely one way to do that.

Cultures of Philosophy

Let us now turn to my narrower, self-imposed brief, that is the relation between educational philosophies and cultures of philosophy. Socrates was a philosopher but, unlike his most famous pupil, he did not have or construct a philosophy. One can philosophize without producing a philosophy, in the same way as one can make music without producing a musical. A philosophy is a more-or-less systematic account of reality, our place within it and how we should comport ourselves towards it. The same distinction can be made between philosophy of education and educational philosophies. Plato and Dewey advanced educational philosophies. Professor X, who devotes himself full-time to analysing the concepts of teaching and learning, does not. An educational philosophy, in my sense, is a more-or-less systematic account of what education is, what its proper aims are, how those aims are legitimately achieved, the relation of education to the wider society, and the location of all this within a broader philosophical picture of the world and the human condition. Plato presents us with an educational philosophy *par excellence* when he tells us that education is a 'turning round' of the soul, aimed at knowledge of the 'Good' and to be achieved by training in maths and dialectic – an account which he relates to the socio-political conditions at once required and promoted by such an education – and he embeds this within a total vision of reality and the human soul. John Dewey also had an educational philosophy, as do Richard Peters, Paul Hirst and John White (see below for more on that subject).

My expression 'cultures of philosophy' is intended to have a Hegelian resonance. There are two aspects of the enterprise of philosophy which Hegel emphasized and which I want to bring out. First, and rather obviously, that enterprise does not take place in a vacuum. The form that it takes in any age is intertwined with the wider culture of the age. Not only does it reflect political, moral, religious, educational and other tendencies of the time, it bears the stamp of other intellectual enquiries (scientific, literary, etc.) simultaneously pursued. It is not simply that these other enquiries serve as fodder for various philosophies of X; they and their methods and 'prejudices' (in Gadamer's sense) shape styles of philosophizing and perceptions of the important issues to address.

Second, less obviously, it can be useful to picture the philosophical enterprise of an age as itself constituting a culture or, better, a complex of cultures – a 'dominant' one, perhaps, and various 'counter-cultures'. The picture highlights the fact that philosophers, like members of cultural groups, have their affiliations and credentials of membership, including the use of particular ideolects, marking themselves off from other groups. It highlights, too, the fact that philosophy is a *tradition* – something, as Heidegger might say, 'always already there', the prevailing moods and styles of which are there to attune to, not the product of individual brains. It highlights the fact that changes in philosophical thinking take place for the same variety of reasons that cultural ones do, for example boredom, fashion, technological innovation, the impact of individual genius and the corrosive influence of rational criticism. The two latter factors are important, because in talking of philosophy as a culture, I am not subscribing to some reductionist, post-modernist image of philosophical enquiry *as nothing but* a social 'conversation' or 'game'. I do not deny that developments in philosophy do sometimes occur for the good reasons that philosophers themselves give. Aristotelian logic required and received revision for the good reasons articulated by Frege and others. However, it would be Utopian to suppose that fashion and the like play nothing of the role they clearly do in other cultural fields, such as art and cuisine.

My expression 'culture of philosophy' is something of a pun. It refers at once to the wider culture in which the philosophical enterprise is enmeshed and to that enterprise as itself something which bears the hallmarks of a culture. So to enquire into the relation between educational philosophies and cultures of philosophy is to ask about the relation of the former to moods and traditions of philosophizing viewed, in part, in their engagement with the wider culture of an age.

Is this relation worth our attention? Can anything interesting and general be said about it? Rather than tackle those questions head on, there follows a 'case-study' to enable us, hopefully, at once to appreciate the importance of the relation and to draw some general lessons about it.

The Case of German Idealism

The great question addressed by Kant and his successors in the age of German Idealism was how to honour and reconcile two unavoidable perspectives which human beings have on themselves – as members of 'the Sensible realm of nature', yet also of 'the supersensible realm of ... freedom' (1966: 2); as 'mere specks' beneath 'the starry heavens', subject to laws of nature, and as intelligences of 'infinite' worth 'independent of the whole world of sense' (1976: 161-162). Kant's question presupposed a whole background of intellectual and cultural developments:

- the decline of a revealed religion which had supplied a confident account of human beings' place in the universe;

- the rise of sciences which at once offered purely naturalistic accounts of human beings yet manifested a rational achievement that seemed sharply to distinguish humans from animal nature;

- educational battles, as registered in *Emile*, over the moral weight of uncorrupted, natural feeling;
- political developments which ranged from embryonic democracies displaying confidence in individual, rational autonomy to nationalistic movements emphasizing individuals' dependence on communities bound together by tradition, myth and *volkisch* sentiment.

If German Idealism was set against a wider cultural context, it can also be viewed as itself constituting something of a culture. Replete with its own poets and artists (for example, Hölderlin and Friedrich), its assumptions shaped the thinking of generations of educated Germans, including such architects of the new *Gymnasien* and universities as Humboldt. Like any culture, the course of its development was the result of factors besides internal philosophical criticism. These included events on the world-stage, notably the wars against Napoleon, with their impact on Fichte's and Hegel's thinking, and currents of social concern which flowed into that 'materialist' counter-culture of philosophy which culminated in Marx.

How was educational thought related to this 'culture of philosophy' (in my dual sense of the expression)? I indicated that educational debate formed part of the cultural setting against which the Idealists formulated their central question, and that Idealist thinking shaped the aims of the educational system which arose in the early nineteenth century. There are two more important points to make. For Kant, famously, it was an inexplicable mystery how we could belong at once to the 'sensible' and 'supersensible' realms, be both subject to nature and yet free. The response of some, above all the playwright and philosopher Friedrich Schiller, was to 'concretise' the problem by seeing it as a *practical* one to be solved through education. Whatever the theoretical difficulties in reconciling people's opposing perspectives on themselves, this opposition is a tragic one, responsible for a contemporary mood of alienation and barbarism. Neither through mere philosophizing nor through political panaceas can this 'division within the inner man' be closed. This can be achieved only though an 'aesthetic education', whereby, in the creative activities Schiller called 'play', the two aspects of our being – our freedom and our material, sensory nature – are harmonized (1967).

Not only did Schiller develop an educational philosophy that 'concretized' the Kantian question, but in so doing he profoundly shaped the future course of Idealist thought. Schelling, for example, agreed that it was through art, in a broad sense, that one should seek unity – a unity which defied theoretical articulation – between the two sides of our being. For Hegel, too, any theoretical solution remains merely 'abstract' unless embodied in the political, artistic and educational forms of a society, in which men and women can truly experience themselves as unities. Hence, *inter alia*, the quest by Humboldt and his colleagues for an education which would promote the 'inner beauty' of the 'whole man'.

What this brief 'case-study' illustrates is something general, namely:

- educational debate as part of the cultural context in which the dominant philosophical issues of an age are articulated;
- the way in which those issues may themselves be 'concretized' as educational ones in the hope of rendering them amenable to solution;
- the manner in which that 'concretization' itself shapes a philosophical culture's course of development;
- the reciprocal impact of that culture on educational policy.

The Dominant Contemporary Culture of Philosophy

Before I inquire into the prospects, in the contemporary context, for emulating Schiller (for fruitfully 'concretizing' large philosophical issues in educational terms and, thereby, influencing their subsequent treatment), I must first sketch my perception of how educational philosophies have been related to the culture of philosophy in modern times.

It might seem that there hasn't been much relation, as the idea that philosophers (including educational ones) should be concocting philosoph*ies* has had a bad press during much of the twentieth century. Peters spoke of the embarrassment professional philosophers now experience when asked 'What is your philosophy of education?', an expression redolent of the 'undifferentiated mush' which educational theory had for so long been (1966: 7 and 15). Ten years earlier, O'Connor asserted that 'having' a philosophy of education, like 'having' one of life, has almost no connection with philosophy in its 'technical meaning', which is purely an activity of 'criticism or clarification', not any body of knowledge and values (1957:2 *et seq.*).

Yet it seems clear that Peters advanced an educational philosophy in my sense, so that either this sense differs from his or, to a degree, his own practice did not entirely accord with his perception of it. It is probably a little of each. Certainly, it is hard to see why his own statement of educational aims was not something he apparently decried, a 'formulation of high-level directives which would guide educational practice' (1966: 15). For the purposes here, O'Connor's case is the more instructive. Not only, *malgré lui*, did his book betray a certain educational philosophy (including a commitment, officially off-limits to a philosopher in the 'technical' sense, to a number of educational aims), but also a larger positivist allegiance which in retrospect appears every bit as metaphysical as the positions attacked under that heading by the positivists. (F.H. Bradley once remarked that those who dismiss the possibility of metaphysics are always peddling a rival one.) What makes this instructive is that positivism was but an extreme version of what, surely, has become the dominant culture of philosophy in twentieth-century English-language circles.

I'll call this the culture of 'naturalism', having toyed with the label 'scientism', one which, however, is perhaps best confined to the kind of *bald* or *reductionist* naturalism which, for example, identifies the mind with the brain or morality with a socio-biological survival kit. Many philosophers of our times certainly embrace that position, but naturalism is a broader church, central to it as scientific enquiry and authority always are. Characteristic of naturalism at large are at least the following tenets:

- the world is the natural world as depictable, in principle, by the natural sciences;

- human beings are entirely natural elements within that world;
- as value and meaning are not entertained by natural scientific enquiry, they constitute no part of the world, but are, say, 'projections' onto it by those unusual creatures, us;
- the realm of knowledge is exhausted by knowing that certain things are the case and by knowing how to do things, as there is no room in the naturalistic account of the world and ourselves for an understanding of the way of things which *eo ipso* bears with it a 'skill in living';
- understanding should be understood as it paradigmatically is among scientists, in terms of submission to canons and criteria endorsed in a community of enquirers in which public, open debate reigns;
- an important ideal – this time not 'projected', but implicit in an exemplary way in scientific practice – is that of rational autonomy of mind, achievable (unparadoxically) through participation in public, criteria-governed modes of enquiry.

This characterization of naturalism will have been a bad one if you do not recognize in it the dominant culture of philosophy of our times, various as the subcultures or currents of thought embraced by it certainly are. It is not simply that many philosophers subscribe to the views sketched here; naturalism also shapes the policy of publishers and journal editors, and those who propound alternative views must necessarily 'take on' naturalism, define their position against it, sometimes achieving fame or notoriety in the process. One distinguished US philosopher goes further. He writes that 'the flood of projects' to fit everything into 'a naturalistic picture of the world' has 'more in common with political or religious ideology than with philosophy' which honours 'the difference between what is known and what is speculated' (Burge, 1993: 117). As with any culture, shifts within the naturalist 'research programme' are liable to influences from outside as well as to internal criticism – consider the impact on philosophers' preoccupations of the lurch from 'behaviourist' to 'cognitive' predilections in psychology. It goes without saying that naturalism has thrived in a wider culture that inspired the problems it addresses and favours the solutions it offers. Above all, one thinks of the remarkable successes (theoretical and technological) of the sciences themselves, the continuing erosion of religious belief, and the corrosive impact of terrible wars and increasing intercourse with other peoples on the confidence in objective moral norms. The story has been told many times.

Unsurprisingly, this culture of philosophy has been reflected in philosophy of education. This was obvious, it was suggested above, with a position like O'Connor's that restricted philosophy of education to the clarification of the concepts and methods of those sciences – the only true suppliers of knowledge – which especially bear on education, and to training an eagle-eye for confusions between factual and evaluative judgements. However, less explicitly, this culture was also partly reflected in the positions of Peters and Paul Hirst. Justly or not, they are sometimes criticized nowadays for conservatism in treating knowledge and understanding in terms of 'initiation' into established disciplines of enquiry, and for an overemphasis of an educational ideal of rational autonomy. Yet precisely that conservatism and ideal, harnessed together, were, we saw, important ingredients of a naturalistic culture which elevates the kind of rational enquiry paradigmatically pursued in the disciplines of science.

The Phenomenological Standpoint

Although what I have called naturalism is today's dominant culture of philosophy, it is not the only one. One thinks, for example, of that loose package of ideas that goes by the name of post-modernism – best thought of, perhaps, as an application to all claims to knowledge, scientific included, of the point the positivists used to make about moral and religious claims – that they are exercises in poetry or rhetoric. It would be interesting to reflect both on the influence on post-modern thinking of *avant-garde* educational theories and on the impact of that thinking, in such guises as 'constructivist mathematics', on current pedagogic trends. However, space is limited, and it is to another counter-culture of philosophy that we now turn in order to offer some thoughts on the potential contemporary role of educational philosophy.

Two striking 'growth areas' in recent years have been aesthetics and environmental philosophy. The connection is not accidental, because interest in both areas indicates dissatisfaction with the naturalistic culture of philosophy. In both aesthetic experience and that of the nature about us – which may sometimes be one and the same – it has struck many writers that there are keys to a human relationship with the world not encompassed by naturalism. In the case of environmental philosophy, this thought has sometimes prompted a drift into *super*naturalism – a 'New Age' vision of the world as divinely or spiritually imbued, as living Gaia. However, I am concerned not with this brand of hostility towards naturalism, but with the kind associated with an increasingly respectable 'continental' import.

'Phenomenology' was the name given by Edmund Husserl to a style of philosophical enquiry which he explicitly contrasted with naturalism. For Husserl, and still more for such followers as Merleau-Ponty and Heidegger, phenomenology focuses on our pre-theoretical experience of and engagement with the 'life-world' (our environment, workplace, artworks, etc.) with the aim of showing what these reveal about our understanding of the world and ourselves, up to and including a (normally implicit) understanding of our place in the order of things.

At every step, the phenomenological standpoint conflicts with the tenets of naturalism. The world is not the one described by natural science, but the human world, the 'life-world'. Scientific descriptions, important for certain purposes, are given their due, but there can be no reason to regard these as more fundamental or authoritative than those of, say, the painter. We are related to the world, first and foremost, not as some natural items causally connected to others, but as agents to a 'field of significance', a vast network of things which stand out for us by virtue of our active, purposeful engagement with them. Value and meaning are not 'projected' or 'conferred', because to experience things is to experience them as mattering and signifying by virtue of that same engagement. Our basic form of understanding is neither the grasp of a body of truths nor a wealth of 'know-how'. Instead, it resides in a shared interpretation or sense of significance implicit in our engagement with the world. Consequently, the paradigm of understanding is not the 'professional' kind obtained from 'disciplines'. To take Merleau-Ponty's example, the more 'primordial' understanding of the forest, from which all others are abstractions, is that of the person who dwells in it, not that of the geographer or botanist (1981: Preface).

Finally, rational autonomy, in so far as it is an ideal at all, is not a function of initiation into disciplines, but the taking up of a reflective stance towards the modes of interpretation that structure our engagement with the world, our 'form of life' in Wittgenstein's famous phrase.

The issue boils down to one of *primacy*. Which have priority, descriptions of a human world as experienced and encountered in everyday life, or ones from an 'objective', theoretical viewpoint? Do the latter tell us how things really and fundamentally are, or do they simply offer information, valuable for certain purposes, but no more privileged than that offered from quite different perspectives? The aim here is not to settle that issue, but to discuss the possible contribution to the debate of reflections on education.

Fortunately, the ground for this discussion has been admirably prepared by John White in his inaugural lecture, *Education and Personal Well-Being in a Secular Universe*. A striking feature of that lecture is the recommendation of an unusually large role in education for the cultivation of a sense of aesthetic and environmental or 'nature-directed' values. The reason for this, which corresponds to the motive behind the attention recently paid to aesthetics and environment in philosophy at large, is that 'we need a vision of education in which our attachment to the *experienced world* is placed centre-stage' (1995b: 19, emphasis added). Why? White's answer is that, with the demise of a religious framework, the young are left 'without bearings'. Told that a certain activity or enquiry is important, children remain without any 'cosmic framework' and, hence, any large picture of human well-being by reference to which they can adjudicate anything's importance. It is White's informed guess that the place to look for such a framework in the secular age is our experience, aesthetic included, of the environment as it impinges on us, with everything that reflection on such experience, unprejudiced by theory, reveals about our relation to the universe as a whole.

On one point, I suggest, White's position needs correcting or at least reformulating. The contemporary educational scene is not, as he says, 'frameworkless', because its framework is surely what I have been calling naturalism. This is easy to overlook, as there is something peculiarly self-effacing about that framework. Having erected it, the naturalists then exit the stage, leaving the real business of telling us about the world, ourselves and how to achieve what we want, to the scientists, their emulators in other disciplines and the technologists. White's complaint can then be rephrased: what leaves children (and their parents) 'without bearings' is not the absence of a framework, but the dominance of one which, by its very character (its portrait of a world without value and significance) is incapable of providing bearings. It is a framework which emerges from reflection on *experienced* nature – the one Bradley said we 'live', with its 'beauty ... terror ... and majesty' (1969: 437), not nature as described in the sciences. In my terminology, it is the nature, not of the naturalists but of the phenomenologists, to which attention must be given.

For my purposes, the central point is not so much the informed guess that it is to aesthetic and environmental experience that we should turn, but more the wider insistence that education should focus on the '*experienced* world' and the 'framework' implicit therein if the young are not to be left 'without bearings' and a reflective conception of wellbeing. Without that focus, the world – the one that figures in theories – becomes, as Heidegger put it, 'dimmed down to [a] uniformity' (1980: 177). A small but apposite example is supplied by Wittgenstein, when he complains of how, in our schools today, children are taught that water is just H_2O and that they are stupid if they don't know that. Thereby, says Wittgenstein, 'the most important questions', for example about water's place in human lives and its roles in sacrament and play, 'are concealed' (1980: 71).

Conclusion

Attending to a pernicious educational dimension of a prevailing culture of thought is, of course, important, but how can it contribute to the philosophical debate between naturalists and their opponents? As Nietzsche taught, truth may be harsh, so a position is not rendered false by having unwelcome consequences. After all, someone might urge, an education conducted within a traditional religious framework may be the most conducive to human well-being, but that hardly demonstrates the truth of the religion.

Yet that analogy is a bad one, at least if a religion is thought of, primarily, as a set of doctrines which, if true, contradicts physics or biology. Although one can indeed not decide on the truth of such doctrines by considering their educational pay-off, matters are less clear when dealing with the conflict between naturalism and phenomenology. Here, the issue is not one of the truth of the sciences, but of their primacy – of the naturalist's claim that they provide a fundamental, objective account of the world. Still, the question remains: how can reflections on education, its aims and failures, intervene in that issue? Perhaps there is something in the thought of the US Pragmatists – James, Dewey and, latterly, Hilary Putnam – that when it comes to deciding between whole philosophical standpoints, questions of value legitimately intervene. A standpoint which registers and reinforces a bad culture or 'form of life' (including its educational ambitions) is properly abandoned and only an artificial dichotomy between ethics and epistemology prevents people from recognizing this.

The aim here is to pursue a more particular thought, although it may be one the Pragmatists were getting at. Naturalism is nothing new; in the eighteenth century versions of it had their champions and critics. Goethe, recalling his student days, tells how the materialism of many Enlightenment thinkers 'appeared to us so grey ... so corpse-like' as to be without relevance to the lives of the students (Copleston, 1985: 50). His friend, Herder, remarked that a person would have to sacrifice his 'humanity' to accept the materialism of his day (1969: 200). Their point might be expressed like this: materialism, or more widely naturalism, cannot be *lived*. Now combine that point with the thought that a philosophy which cannot be 'lived' – at any rate, one that 'living' contradicts – cannot, for that very reason, be credible. It cannot, that is, be one which anyone who 'lives' may seriously and consistently endorse, however much 'lip-service' is paid to it. In that case, the 'unliveability' of a philosophical standpoint becomes a genuine objection to it, a reason for rejecting it.

Now, by 'living' here is not meant simply chugging along and managing not to expire, rather the shaping of one's life and the taking of those paths and large decisions which give life its direction and, in a sense, define who one is, one's conception of oneself. If, then, we are to enquire into the idea that naturalism is incredible because unliveable, it is fairly clear where we should focus. It is instructive that Goethe was writing of his student days, because the issues of living, as characterized, although not the prerogative of youth, are at their most salient during that stage on life's way. None of the more mature among us, I imagine, would like to think of ourselves as just chugging along – there is, after all, such a thing as 'lifelong learning' – but most of the paths and decisions giving our lives direction and shape were taken long ago. We are to a large extent what we have been.

So the question to ask is: can our young people 'live' the naturalist standpoint? If they cannot, then it is not one they can seriously accept and nor can we, as we once 'lived' as well and, therefore, cannot subscribe to a view which makes that happy period incomprehensible. I take John White's argument, as I revamped it, to be that they (and we) cannot 'live' this standpoint. Naturalism – the framework for so much contemporary education – leaves the young without the bearings required for taking these rather than those paths in life, for directing their lives in this rather than that way.

Yet this can be challenged. Quite clearly the young of today – and of any day – do take paths and make life-shaping decisions, of career, sexual behaviour, political allegiance and so on. Yet one shouldn't conclude that, after all, naturalism is compatible with 'living'. To the extent that young people really are *taking* paths and *making* decisions, not just drifting into this or that 'lifestyle', this may simply show that the naturalistic standpoint has not taken complete hold of them. As a proponent and a perceptive critic of naturalism, John Mackie and Iris Murdoch, respectively, point out, from the naturalistic standpoint *all* experience of the rightness or wrongness, the beauty or ugliness, the significance or insignificance of what there is in the world is in *error*, because the naturalists' world contains nothing answering to such experience. It follows that anyone who takes paths and decisions in the light of such experience does so in error and has not yet internalized the naturalists' message. If *that* is the reason the young are not yet *entirely* without bearings, this is hardly any defence of naturalism.

The naturalist will say that I am ignoring an alternative: the paths followed by the young need not be ones they simply drift into or ones they follow in the light of erroneous experience. They can, and should, be ones they simply *choose* autonomously. Or more accurately, they should be ones dictated by values autonomously chosen. The young are not left without bearings, but with only those bearings for which they themselves elect. This idea of values as choices, as the products of so many *actes gratuits*, is probably incoherent, but it is anyway surely unfaithful to our experience of value and significance. I choose in the light of how things already present themselves and matter to me, not vice-versa. There is no space to argue that point here, but if well-taken the conclusion must be that naturalism indeed leaves the young without bearings – that it is therefore unliveable and so incredible. Bearings can be supplied only by reflection on a pre-theoretical experience of the 'lived world' of a kind demoted, or even dismissed as erroneous, by naturalism.

I have argued that educational philosophy can be more than an application of wider philosophy to a field of human activity. By 'concretizing' issues which preoccupy that wider culture of philosophy in educational terms, light can be cast on those issues. Taking my cue from John White, I have argued, in particular, that attention to the failure of the climate of contemporary education to provide or refuse the bearings by which young people might live indicates, in a salient way, the incredibility of a broad perspective that constitutes the dominant philosophical culture of our times. My argument may be wrong, but unless it is plain silly, I have shown that educational philosophy can legitimately intervene in and contribute to the larger culture of philosophy. Hopefully, that does something to restore to the subject some of its 'lost dignity'.

References

Bradley, F.H. (1969), *Appearance and Reality*. Oxford: Oxford University Press.

Burge, T. (1993) in J. Heil & A. Mele (eds), *Mental Causation*. Oxford: Oxford University Press.

Copleston, F. (1985), *A History of Philosophy, Vol. 6*. New York: Image.

Dewey, J. (1946), *Democracy and Education*. New York: Free Press.

Heidegger, M. (1980), *Being and Time*. Oxford: Blackwell.

Herder, J.G. (1969), *On Social and Political Culture*. Cambridge: Cambridge University Press.

Kant, I. (1966), *Critique of Judgement*. New York: Hafner.

— (1976), *Critique of Practical Reason*. Indianapolis: Bobbs-Merrill.

Merleau-Ponty, M. (1981), *Phenomenology of Perception*. London: Routledge & Kegan Paul.

O'Connor, D.J. (1957), *An Introduction to the Philosophy of Education*. London: Routledge & Kegan Paul.

Peters, R.S. (1966), *Ethics and Education*. London: Allen & Unwin.

Plato (1961), *Republic in Collected Dialogues*. Princeton: Princeton University Press.

Schiller, F. (1967), *On the Aesthetic Education of Man*. Oxford: Oxford University Press.

Siegel, H. (1990), *Educating Reason*. New York: Routledge.

White, J.P. (1995a), 'Education, problems of the philosophy of' in T. Honderich (ed.), *The Oxford Companion to Philosophy*. Oxford: Oxford University Press.

— (1995b), *Education and Personal Well-Being in a Secular Universe.* London: Institute of Education.

Winch, C. (1996), *Quality and Education.* Oxford: Blackwell.

Wittgenstein, L. (1980), *Culture and Value.* Oxford: Blackwell.

3 De-moralizing Education

Susan Mendus

Introduction

What does education in liberal democratic societies such as ours offer its students by way of moral guidance, and what should it offer? This is the question which I wish to address, and it is a question which is prominent both in British society generally and in moral and political philosophy more specifically. Thus, in her recent, and much discussed book, *All Must Have Prizes*, Melanie Phillips states that it is her task to:

> discover how, in an age of unparalleled scientific progress and material prosperity, we have de-moralized our society and put at risk some of our most priceless assets ... we have devalued our children's education: a process not merely of intellectual collapse but of moral disintegration which now threatens the survival of our culture.
>
> (1996: xiv)

Phillips' allegation is that society in general, and teachers in particular, have reneged on their responsibility to instil moral values in those they educate and that, as a result, students are left with no sense of what is morally right and wrong beyond what they themselves choose or prefer:

> The young have been taught ... that they should never think of the views of others as false, but only as different. They have been taught that to suggest that someone else is wrong is at best rude and at worst immoral: the truth that one should always be alive to the possibility that one is wrong has become the falsehood that one should never be so arrogant as to believe that one is right.
>
> (1996: 221, quoting Marianne Talbot)

The picture which Phillips paints – and deplores – is one of a world in which we lack confidence in our own moral beliefs, are impotent in the face of conflicting moral beliefs, and are fearful of the responsibility of transmitting our morality to the next generation. In short, we have become like Robert Frost's liberals – people who are afraid to take their own side in an argument.

Moreover, Phillips has weighty philosophical allies. In his important work of moral and political philosophy, *Whose Justice? Which Rationality?*, Alasdair MacIntyre provides the following description of education in modern liberal societies such as Britain and the United States:

> What the student is confronted with ... is an apparent inconclusiveness in all argument outside the natural sciences, an inconclusiveness which seems to abandon him or her to his or her prerational preferences. So the student characteristically emerges from a liberal education with a set of skills, a set of preferences, and little else, someone whose education has been as much a process of deprivation as of enrichment.
>
> (1988: 400)

The message is clear: what education should offer is a defence, explanation or justification of substantive moral values. Indeed of *our* moral values. What it in fact offers is simply a liquorice allsorts of rival and competing moralities between which the individual student is invited to choose, but in the choice of which he or she is given no useful guidance.

Finally, and perhaps most famously, Allan Bloom argues in his cult book, *The Closing of the American Mind*, that:

> there is one thing a professor can be absolutely certain of: almost every student entering the university believes, or says he believes, that truth is relative ... the relativity of truth is not a theoretical insight but a moral postulate, the condition of a free society, or so they see it ... relativism is necessary to openness and this is the virtue, the only virtue, which all primary education for more than 50 years has dedicated itself to inculcating.
> (1987: 25-26)

All three writers (Phillips, MacIntyre and Bloom) concur in thinking that modern education fails society and fails its students by construing moral judgement as a matter of arbitrary, even capricious, personal opinion in a world in which any opinion is as good, or as bad, as any other. According to their view, teachers are, or should be, charged with the task of communicating and defending the moral values of the community, but teachers are so impressed by the diversity of moral belief within the community, and so seized of the importance of tolerating that diversity, that they now believe that moral relativism is the only game in town.

If this analysis of modern educational practice is true (and I think there is certainly some truth in it), it is important to understand *why* it is true. Whether teachers are or are not committed to moral relativism, they are certainly reluctant to engage in the inculcation of substantive moral values, and this in itself is interesting. It is also comparatively new. In doing the background reading for this chapter, I came across the Proceedings of the First International Moral Education Congress held at the University of London in September, 1908. Of the 124 contributions to the Congress, not one raised the question of whether moral values should be taught. That they should was taken for granted, and so discussion centred on how best to discharge the task in hand.

All this has now changed, and the question of whether moral values should be taught at all has become one of the burning issues of educational policy and practice. I have already alluded to three writers who see the reluctance to teach moral values as something which has lamentable consequences both for students themselves and for society at large. At the same time, however, many teachers are resistant to the suggestion that they should become the moral mentors of their students. So democratic societies, such as Britain, are societies in which, at the same time, the demand that moral values be taught is matched only by the reluctance to teach them.

The following will attempt to explain why this unstable combination of tendencies is present, and, therefore, why there is a gap between what education does offer and what (on some understandings) it can and should offer. My suggestion will be that there are two pertinent sets of facts, namely facts about the world and facts about us in that world, which make it imperative that moral values be taught and also almost impossible to teach them. In conditions of modernity, the teaching of moral values is something which we desperately need but cannot have.

First, I will draw attention to those facts about the world, and about us, which appear to make the teaching of moral values both necessary and impossible. Second, I will consider what the causes of this conundrum might be. Finally, I will make some positive (although tentative) suggestions as to how the conundrum might be addressed, solved, or resolved.

Facts about the World

In his most recent book, *Political Liberalism*, John Rawls (1993) claims that modern democratic societies are confronted by problems quite different from those which arose in earlier, pre-modern times, and that these different problems have their origin in (but are not confined to) changed understandings of religion. Rawls writes:

> When moral philosophy began, say with Socrates, ancient religion was a civic religion of public social practice, of civic festivals and public celebrations. Moreover, this civic religious

culture was not based on a sacred work like the Bible, or the Koran, or the Vedas of Hinduism ... as long as one participated in the expected way and recognized the proprieties, the details of what one believed were not of great importance. It was a matter of doing the done thing and being a trustworthy member of society, always ready to carry out one's civic duties as a good citizen – to serve on juries or to row in the fleet in war – when called upon to do so. It was not a religion of salvation in the Christian sense and there was no class of priests who dispensed the necessary means of grace; indeed the ideas of immortality and eternal salvation did not have a central place in classical culture.

(1993: xxi)

However, Rawls claims, all this changed in the Reformation period, when religion came to be seen as a route to salvation and when, at the same time, adherents of different religions held conflicting beliefs about which route was the correct one. It was no longer the case that religion was a matter of mere 'outward observance' or 'civic duty'. Instead, it was held as, in Rawls' terminology, a 'comprehensive conception'. That is to say, religious belief included an understanding of the morally right way to lead one's life, the way which would lead to salvation and life everlasting. So whereas, in the ancient world, 'the details of what one believed were not of great importance', in the post-Reformation period, what one believes has come to be of paramount importance.

This combination of a salvationist conception of religion and conflicting opinions about how to attain salvation, gave rise (Rawls says) to a new and distinctively modern set of problems in political life. These are problems which survive the specific context in which they arose, and can now be expressed in the quite general question: 'how can there exist over time a just and stable society of free and equal citizens, who remain profoundly divided by reasonable religious, philosophical and moral doctrines?' (1993: xviii). This, for Rawls, is *the* question of modernity, and it is not a question of morality, but one of political stability.

One pertinent fact about our world, then, is that it contains people of different and conflicting religious, moral and philosophical beliefs. Those beliefs are often the most significant things in the lives of their adherents. Certainly they trump political considerations, and are seen as more important than the policies of local education authorities, or the practices of neighbourhood schools. After all, they often refer to the conditions and possibility of life everlasting and, therefore, must take priority over the political and secular prescriptions of the here and now.

Moreover, the problem is heightened when Rawls insists that the facts of pluralism consist not merely in there being different yet conflicting comprehensive conceptions of the good (moral beliefs), but different *yet reasonable* comprehensive conceptions of the good (moral beliefs). He claims that it is not the case that we can simply discard all but one of these opposing views as mad, bad or dangerous to know. Some, of course, might be of that sort, however there will be many comprehensive conceptions which are perfectly reasonable, but which nevertheless conflict with other, equally reasonable, conceptions. Indeed, and interestingly, Rawls does not simply state this as a contingent fact about societies such as Britain and the United States. He makes a stronger claim, which is that the existence of conflicting yet reasonable moral views is the predictable outcome of the operation of reason under conditions of freedom. The facts of pluralism are facts which follow inevitably and necessarily from the deployment of reason, and therefore 'to see reasonable pluralism as a disaster is to see the exercise of reason under the conditions of freedom itself as a disaster' (1993: xxiv).

This gives us four significant facts about the modern world:

- it is a world in which moral and religious belief is of paramount importance to many people;
- it is a world in which moral and religious beliefs conflict one with another;
- it is a world in which the conflict may be a conflict between *reasonable* moral beliefs;
- it is a world in which that conflict cannot be expected to go away.

The educational implications of this are two-fold. First, the co-existence of reasonable yet conflicting comprehensive conceptions of the good makes the demand to teach moral values difficult to satisfy. If there really are conflicting yet reasonable views, how are we to decide which ones are to be taught? The second consequence, however, is that moral values themselves become, in a sense, of secondary importance in such societies. This is because divergence is, on Rawls' account, the natural outcome of the operation of reason, and also because the crucial and pressing question is not how we can agree in our moral judgements (that is not a serious possibility on Rawls' account), but how we can live with persistent disagreement. (How we can live together even though we have conflicting opinions about the morally right way to live.)

Against this background, Rawls urges that, as far as possible, education should distance itself from questions of morality and concentrate on teaching political skills. He writes:

> Justice as fairness does not seek to cultivate the distinctive virtues and values of the liberalisms of autonomy and individuality, or indeed of any other comprehensive doctrine ... we try to answer the question of children's education entirely within the political conception. Society's concern with their education lies in their role as future citizens, and so in such essential things as their acquiring the capacity to understand the public culture and to participate in its institutions.
> (1993: 199-200)

There is an important *caveat* here, of course, which is that democratic societies cannot endorse those moral beliefs (comprehensive conceptions) which deny the legitimacy of democratic liberalism itself, but beyond that, positive efforts should be made to refrain from inculcating any particular set of moral values (any comprehensive conception). Presumably, what this means is that educational policy should not require teachers to take a stance on controversial moral issues (such as abortion, euthanasia, the propriety of monogamous marriage, the authority of the Koran, the Bible or any other sacred text), except and insofar as these doctrines threaten to undermine the workings of democracy itself. In brief, and for Rawls, substantive moral education, beyond what is necessary for the stability of democracy, is something which we cannot have, should not expect and need not hanker after.

To summarize so far, then, my suggestion is that in modern democratic societies such as Britain and the United States, the teaching of moral values is both imperative and impossible. That it is so follows from a combination of facts about the world and facts about us. The facts about the world, as presented in Rawls' *Political Liberalism*, are ones which imply that the teaching of substantive moral values is impossible, because we cannot know which of the many and conflicting moral values we should teach, and because a decision to teach any one set would jeopardize political stability. Our problem now is *not* to create a community of kindred spirits in which moral values are accepted and agreed upon (contrast Melanie Phillips on this), but to live together despite our deep, yet reasonable, differences about moral values. These, then, are the facts about the world. What of the facts about us in that world?

Facts about Us

Whereas Rawls concentrates on a central *political* problem of modernity (the problem of stability), other writers have concentrated on what we might call an *existential* problem of modernity. One of the most prominent of these writers is Charles Taylor who, in *Sources of the Self*, claims that we are in:

> A fundamentally different existential predicament from that which dominated most previous cultures and still defines the lives of other people today. That alternative is a predicament in which an unchallengeable framework makes imperious demands which we fear being unable to meet. We face the prospect of irretrievable condemnation or exile, of being marked down in obloquy forever, or of being sent to damnation irrevocably ...

the form of danger here is utterly different from that which
threatens the modern seeker, which is something close to the
opposite: the world loses altogether its spiritual contour, nothing
is worth doing, the fear is of a terrifying emptiness, a kind of
vertigo, or even a fracturing of our world and body-space.

(1989: 18)

So, where Rawls insists that the facts of pluralism are not a disaster, but merely the inevitable outcome of the operation of reason under conditions of freedom, Taylor takes those same facts to be ones which can deliver us (existentially) into a state of anomie and meaninglessness ('the world loses altogether its spiritual contour, nothing is worth doing').

Interestingly, both agree that we can no longer expect to live in a homogeneous society, where a single set of moral or religious values has the status of unquestionable truth. However, whereas Rawls denies that this is a cause for lamentation and sees it instead as a compelling reason for giving centre stage to questions of politics (especially of political stability), Taylor sees it as the single most important factor contributing to our sense of rootlessness and meaninglessness. Put crudely, he claims that in a world where a single set of moral or religious beliefs commands universal assent, and especially where those beliefs draw their authority from God or from something which transcends human beings and human desires, we may suffer from a sense of moral inadequacy or moral failure, but we will not suffer from a sense that nothing matters morally. This, however, is precisely the *malaise* of modernity – confronted by a vast array of different and conflicting sets of moral beliefs, none of which commands unquestionable assent, we find ourselves cast into a void where moral beliefs can only be a matter of decision for us, and we are conspicuously inadequate to the task of deciding.

Similar anxieties are expressed by Alasdair MacIntyre, who notes that, having abandoned belief in God and placed our faith in the power of our own reason, we find that reason can deliver only a cacophony of conflicting moral voices. Thus, we argue interminably and fruitlessly about such moral questions as the permissibility of abortion, the nature of justice and the moral status of war (to name but three), and the problem is not simply that these debates go on and on – although they do – but also that they apparently can find no terminus. 'There seems', says MacIntyre, 'to be no rational way of securing agreement in our culture' (1981: 6). For MacIntyre, it is not simply that we cannot as a matter of fact agree about whether, for example, abortion is morally wrong. Rather, we cannot even agree about what would *count* as a satisfactory resolution of the problem, and different people with differing moral frameworks will have conflicting views even about what constitutes evidence in favour of one conclusion rather than another.

Where Taylor's concern is that this leaves us in a moral void, MacIntyre is more concerned to point out that it also leaves us 'betrayed' by our moral language. For MacIntyre, what is most significant about reason's failure to secure agreement is that we do not, on the whole, recognize that failure. Thus, we speak and act as if moral judgements had authority (as if they expressed a truth about the matter in hand), but we have in fact abandoned or otherwise lost the conditions under which they could express any such truth or hold any such authority. 'Hence,' he concludes, 'the slightly shrill tone of so much moral debate' (1981: 8).

All three of the writers considered here (Rawls, Taylor and MacIntyre) agree that human reason will not, and cannot, deliver agreement on moral matters, but their views have dramatically different implications for the teaching of moral values. Rawls concludes that, as moral agreement is something we cannot have, and as it is not even something we can legitimately want, we must accept our moral differences and concentrate on the promotion of political stability. What political stability requires of us in an educational context is that we should, so far as possible, abstain from taking any position on moral values. By contrast, Taylor and MacIntyre, in different ways, see the facts of moral fragmentation and disagreement as facts deeply damaging to us as individuals and to society as a whole – on Taylor's account they leave us morally bereft, whereas on MacIntyre's account they leave us morally betrayed. If we take seriously the claim that reason cannot deliver moral agreement, and if there really are diverse and conflicting, yet reasonable moral beliefs, how are we to avoid a sense that it does not matter which we choose (*ex hypothese* they are all reasonable), and therefore that morality itself does not matter? This is Taylor's question.

Conversely, how are we to justify any sense that some things *do* matter and that, for example, the violation of human rights or the wilful destruction of human life are morally wrong? This is MacIntyre's question and the force of his claim that in the modern world we are 'betrayed' by our moral language, because we speak and act as if there were human rights and as if their violation were a matter of supreme importance, but our acceptance of diverse and conflicting moral views robs us of the resources necessary to justify that claim to importance. Combining the insights of MacIntyre and Taylor delivers a picture of moral belief as either meaningless or fraudulent. And it is the necessity of extricating ourselves from this predicament which makes the teaching of moral values imperative in MacIntyre's eyes.

My aim so far has been to show why it is the case that moral education is something we both need and cannot have. We need to inculcate moral values in students in order to dispel the belief that morality is no more than a matter of arbitrary choice between conflicting alternatives. At the same time, we cannot justify the claim that morality really is more than a matter of arbitrary choice between conflicting alternatives. That it is more than that is certainly something we want to believe and our moral language bears testimony to that desire (we speak as if our moral judgements had authority). It is not, however, something which we are entitled to believe, and, therefore, we are faced with the dark possibility that morality is at best an inadequate guide to the journey we must make in our lives, and at worst a positively misleading map of the terrain we will traverse.

Facts about the World and Facts about Us

Is there, then, any possibility of reconciling these two opposing sets of considerations and creating a world in which we can have what we both want and need? Can the teaching of substantive moral values be justified in a way which will deliver us from moral meaninglessness or moral betrayal, but which, at the same time, will not threaten political stability by undermining the reasonable moral beliefs which conflict with those which are officially taught? Let me say now that I don't think I can square this circle, and the aim here is not to solve the problem, but to indicate just how deep and intransigent it is. Whatever the solution to our existential, moral and political difficulties, it cannot be simply a matter of embracing old-fashioned (or even new-fangled) moral beliefs and inculcating them in our students. For reasons which Rawls identifies, it is a very significant part of our problem that we live in a society replete with diverse and conflicting, yet reasonable, moral views. Therefore, the solution cannot be to ignore that diversity and to require teachers to inculcate one specific set of values on the spurious and ultimately duplicitous grounds that they are, in some way, 'ours'. So, what are the prospects?

Rawls, Taylor and MacIntyre all agree that, in the modern world, reason delivers moral diversity, not moral unanimity. Of course, they differ dramatically in their evaluation of this state of affairs, but that it is the state of affairs is not an issue between them. However, there could be a number of different explanations for reason's failure to deliver unanimity, with different implications for the possibility of teaching moral values. I will discuss two of these – the claim that reason fails to deliver agreement about moral values because moral values are themselves plural, and the claim that reason fails to deliver agreement because reason is incomplete. Just as there were facts about the world and facts about us which prompted the problem, so there are facts about the world and facts about us which may deliver a (partial) solution.

One proposed explanation for reason's inability to deliver agreement on moral matters is that moral values are themselves incompatible with one another. This, if it is a fact at all, is a fact about the world. There are, it is said, many different moral values, not all of which are consistent one with another, and therefore our failure to agree in moral judgement is a consequence of the fact that moral values themselves do not cohere harmoniously. Let us suppose that this is the case. What follows for the teaching of moral values? Some have thought that belief in the incompatibility of moral values (value pluralism) devalues morality and turns it into a matter of 'supermarket choice'. The argument goes something like this: if the world contains multiple and conflicting moral values, then it must simply be up to the individual to decide which values to embrace and act upon. Morality becomes merely a matter of personal choice or preference. This, as was seen above, was the conclusion drawn by Bloom and MacIntyre, both of whom argue that in the modern world moral judgement has been reduced to a matter of mere preference. However, if modern education does reduce morality to a matter of mere preference, that is not, I think, a direct consequence of construing moral values as incompatible.

Consider the case of the tragic hero. Characteristically, he or she is portrayed as someone who is confronted with a choice between different, yet incompatible, values, such that both cannot simultaneously be satisfied. So, Antigone is faced with a choice between burying her brother and obeying the orders of the king, Hamlet is faced with a choice between committing murder and leaving his father's death unavenged, and John Proctor in *The Crucible* is faced with a choice between telling a lie and losing his life. In all these cases, the choice of one valuable thing precludes the choice of another, equally valuable, thing. The incompatibility of values is the very stuff of tragic conflict. However, the correct conclusion to draw from this is not that it does not matter how we choose. On the contrary, it matters a great deal how we choose. Whichever way we choose in the tragic situation, we have done wrong. Far from indicating that moral judgement is trivial and inconsequential, the incompatibility of values can show us that moral judgement is both supremely important and supremely difficult. So the incompatibility of values does not, in itself, lead to the conclusion that morality is merely a matter of opinion in a world in which any opinion is as good as any other.

A second explanation for reason's inability to deliver agreement lies not in a fact about the world and the moral values it contains, but rather in a fact about us. Here, the claim is that reason will not deliver unanimity because reason (that is human reason) is inadequate or incomplete. Again, it is sometimes thought that this heralds the arrival of moral scepticism or relativism – as we cannot know with certainty which of the many moral values is correct, we must hold our own moral views provisionally and give others the benefit of the doubt. Although appeal to the inadequacy of reason may foster that conclusion, it need not do so. Appeal to the inadequacy of reason is quite compatible with the belief that there is a moral truth, and that that moral truth can be known. Indeed, appeal to the inadequacy of reason *implies* that there is a moral truth, but it goes on to point out that we do not, at the moment, know it.

The two proposed explanations for reason's inability to deliver moral agreement are then that we have diverse moral views because there are diverse moral values (it is a fact about the world that it contains incompatible values), and/or we have diverse moral views because we have incomplete understanding (it is a fact about us that we cannot yet make those values combine harmoniously). I have suggested that neither of these need lead to moral relativism or scepticism, neither need imply that morality is merely a matter of personal preference or that any moral opinion is as good as any other. It is in fact quite the reverse, in that the incompatibility of values is what provides us with a sense of the tragic, not of the trivial. The inadequacy of reason implies that there is moral truth, not that we must be moral sceptics or moral relativists. Nevertheless, these two sets of considerations have implications both for the possibility of moral education and for the manner in which it can properly be conducted. What are those implications?

Summary and Conclusions

My starting point was the contention that, in the modern world, the teaching of moral values appears to be both imperative and impossible: impossible because, given the facts of pluralism, favouring one set of moral values over another would be unjustifiable and also a threat to political stability. At the same time, however, the teaching of moral values seems to be imperative because the facts of pluralism also leave us existentially without moral anchorage. In a plural world, we cannot justifiably alight upon a single set of moral values as the ones which must be taught, but we stand in urgent need of some set of moral values which will release us from the sense that 'nothing matters' morally speaking, or that our moral judgements are merely ungrounded preferences.

I have also suggested that these two sets of difficulties (the difficulty of agreeing on moral values and the difficulty of living without agreement on moral values) can be traced to the nature of human reason or to the nature of moral values. Our failure to agree could be a consequence of reason's inadequacy (a fact about us), or it could be a consequence of the incommensurability of values (a fact about the world). In neither case, however, need we be driven to moral scepticism or relativism: our failure to agree need not imply that it does not matter how we choose or that there is no such thing as choosing well or badly. Thus, the tragic case shows that how we choose may be a matter of paramount importance precisely because the choice is a choice between things *of value*. The belief that disagreement can be traced to the inadequacy of reason implies that there is a truth and that we should aim towards it in however stumbling a way.

Where does all this leave the teacher, and what model of moral education does it imply or permit? The arguments considered here suggest one anti-Platonic conclusion and one pro-Platonic conclusion. In the space remaining I will try to say a little about these two.

As is well known, Plato believed that there is a single moral truth, and that that truth is one which we can know. Nevertheless, he denied that it is the task of the teacher to instil that truth into the student. The teacher does not *transmit* knowledge. Rather, he or she should act as the 'midwife's apprentice', as someone who enables students to come to see what they already know but have not yet been able to articulate. In other words, the teacher 'draws out' the knowledge which is already within the student. This aspect of Plato's philosophy cannot, I think, serve as the model for moral education today. The arguments and considerations adduced here militate against an understanding of moral value as unitary, and indeed modern moral and political philosophy emphasize quite the reverse – the diversity and conflicting nature of moral judgement. Against this background, a conception of moral education as the means of eliciting a single, latent moral truth is unpromising, as it is our problem (and, therefore, cannot be our solution) that no single moral truth is discernible. Again, it does not follow from this that there is no moral truth – only that, even if there is a moral truth, we do not know it at the moment.

However, if moral education cannot proceed on the assumption that there is a truth and that we (or some of us) know it, it cannot proceed on the assumption that moral judgement is merely a matter of personal decision or preference either. This is because the conflicting values are conflicting *values*. As the example of tragic conflict makes clear, they are things which matter, not whims or caprices. Indeed it is in this context that R.M. Hare has referred quite generally to the freedom associated with moral judgement as a burdensome freedom – a freedom which, when properly understood, will not leave us feeling liberated to do whatever we wish, but one which is onerous because it carries a heavy responsibility with it:

> Although most of us think that we are free to form our own opinions about moral questions, we do not feel that it does not matter what we think about them – that the answering of moral questions is a quite arbitrary business, like the choice of one postage stamp from the sheet rather than another. We feel, rather, that it matters very much what answer we give, and that the finding of an answer is a task that should engage our rational powers to the limit of their capacity. So the freedom that we have in morals is to be distinguished from the freedom which comes when it simply does not matter what we do or say. That is why, when people grow up to the stage at which they start to understand that in moral questions they are free to form their own opinions, they feel this freedom, not as an emancipation, but as a burden.
>
> (Hare, 1963: 2-3)

Although Hare makes this point in relation to how we should understand our own moral decisions and actions, it also has implications for the role of the teacher in moral education. As we have seen, the teacher must refrain from implying that there is a single moral truth and that he or she possesses it. At the same time, however, the teacher must emphasize that the 'freedom' to make one's own moral decisions is not a matter of emancipation, much less a matter of mere choice or preference. Rather, it is a significant and onerous responsibility. Here we find the second, and more appropriate, Platonic dimension of the problem.

In Book VII of *Republic* Plato emphasizes that only those who are unwilling to enter politics can be trusted with political office. Indeed, he goes further, urging that people (men) who are fitted to rule will have to be coerced and dragooned into doing so. They will not volunteer. One reason for this is that politics offers the opportunity to attain power over others, and those who seek such power show themselves to be suspect just because their motivations are motivations to obtain power, not motivations to govern well. The same can, I think, be said of the teaching of moral values – those who are eager to engage in this task thereby raise the suspicion that they are unsuited for it, and that they wish to impose their own moral views on their students. It must be emphasized that what is wrong with this is not that it implies that there are moral truths to be discerned when in fact 'everything is relative'. As we have seen, Plato was convinced that there are moral truths to be discerned, but he still rejected a model of teaching as the activity of transmitting those truths from teacher to student. So doubts about inculcating moral values are quite independent of any commitment to relativism or scepticism. Rather, what is problematic about the injunction to teach moral values is that such an enterprise, unless carefully undertaken, may undermine the deep and inescapable personal responsibility which lies at the heart of moral judgement. That responsibility emerges acutely in the tragic case, but it exists in all cases of moral decision.

The demand that teachers convey 'our' values (the values of our society) is to be resisted therefore not simply because our society consists of many conflicting sets of moral values, but also because the nature of moral judgement and moral responsibility is such that it rests ultimately with the individual. Whatever my teacher may say, whatever my priest may advise, whatever my counsellor may endorse, in the end I stand alone as the author of my own moral actions and the choice which I make is both a choice between valuable things and a choice which is inescapably mine.

This bleak truth must be conveyed via moral education. It is a truth which transcends debates between objectivists and relativists, which involves more than instruction in critical thinking, but less than the inculcation of substantive moral values. My question was 'what does modern education offer its students by way of moral guidance, and what should it offer?' My answer is that it should offer two things, namely an awareness of the complex and intransigent nature of moral conflict in conditions of modernity, and a recognition that that intransigence does not make the moral responsibility of the individual go away. As a teacher, I have moral values which I believe to be correct, and I wish my students to endorse those values. However, I must also accept that, if they do endorse them, they are themselves responsible for the sometimes tragic consequences which may ensue, and they cannot escape that responsibility by appealing to 'higher authority' or 'what their teacher told them'. I must, therefore, provide a clear account of my own moral beliefs and of why I hold them, but I must also remember that in doing that, I pass on responsibility, not knowledge. To forget this fact is, in more than one sense, to de-moralize education. To remember it is to set the scene for at least another 50 years of philosophy of education.

References

Bloom, A. (1987), *The Closing of the American Mind.* New York: Simon & Schuster (also 1993, Harmondsworth: Penguin).

Hare, R. M. (1963), *Freedom and Reason.* Oxford: Oxford University Press.

MacIntyre A. (1981), *After Virtue.* London: Duckworth.

— (1988), *Whose Justice? Which Rationality?* London: Duckworth.

Phillips, M. (1996), *All Must Have Prizes.* London: Little, Brown.

Rawls, J. (1993), *Political Liberalism.* New York: Columbia University Press.

Taylor, C. (1989), *Sources of the Self.* Cambridge: Cambridge University Press.

4 Educational Research: Re-establishing the Philosophical Terrain

David Bridges

Introduction

It is a very special pleasure and honour for me to be invited to contribute to the celebration of 50 years of philosophy of education at the London Institute of Education, not least because of the personal debt that I feel that I owe to many of those who are part of that history.

My own association with the Institute does not go back quite the whole length of that 50 years, but it does cover two-thirds of that time, as it was in 1963 that I first arrived there as a PGCE student to discover a feast of intellectual excitement which certainly exceeded my previous experience as a history undergraduate at Oxford and which has rarely been equalled since.

My history tutor at the Institute was Jim Henderson, a Jungian who with rich eccentricism offered a view of history teaching as an opportunity to explore the archetypes of the unconscious and who also pioneered the teaching of contemporary world history as a contribution to international peace and understanding. Joseph Lauwerys, a man of enormous synoptic vision, taught me comparative education, and on a Friday morning in the Beveridge Hall Basil Bernstein was savagely dissecting the mechanisms by which schooling reproduced the structures of educational and social disadvantage and was beginning to expound his seminal account of the role of language in this process. Richard Peters was laying out his potent analysis of the inter-connected notions of freedom, authority, equality and democracy and their relation with the concept of education itself – a performance spiced with the occasional effervescent intervention on knowledge and the curriculum by Paul Hirst. I am afraid, however, that all of these were undoubtedly overshadowed by a wonderful lady (whose name has I am afraid not survived in quite the same way as these others) who combined a lecture on health education with a demonstration of the use of visual aids. This included an explanation of the process of human excretion conducted with the aid of a nylon stocking and an orange (and to the accompaniment of the massed grunting of the Beveridge Hall audience) – a height of hilarity only exceeded when, in a subsequent demonstration of the use of the felt board to teach the human reproductive system, a felt representation of the male member was observed slowly to curl over and then drop off the board.

This light relief apart, no-one involved in those days in the initial education of teachers felt any need to apologise for engaging those new teachers with the richest, the most critical and most fertile theoretical perspectives that they could lay their hands on. They expected to extend the minds of postgraduate students as well as their practical competence and they expected them to go out into schools fully confident that they could contribute to the improvement of contemporary educational practice and not merely accommodate to its reproduction. I for one am eternally grateful that the initial training I received was informed by this vision and ambition rather than the requirement that it conform to the pedestrian and bureaucratically informed requirements of a government quango.

> And how can a man teach with authority, which is the life of teaching, how can he be a doctor in his book as he ought to be, or else had better be silent, when as all he teaches, all he delivers, is but under the tuition, under the correction of his patriarchal licenser to blot or alter what precisely accords not with the hidebound humour which he calls his judgement? ... I hate a

pupil teacher, I endure not an instructor that comes to me under the wardship of an overseeing fist.
(Milton, 1644, 1967 edn: 167)

The intellectual excitement came in a different, but still exhilarating form when I returned to the Institute to do the Diploma in Philosophy of Education in 1968 and then the MA and my PhD with Richard Peters. I had studied some 'history of ideas', but had never studied philosophy, and I remember the wonderful sense of iconoclasm and emancipation when Peters replied to one contributor to an early seminar, 'Well, yes, so that is what Plato said, but was he right?' I remember as a brand new student of philosophy sitting down with a piece of paper on which was written the first essay title given to us by John White: 'Are synthetic *a priori* truths possible?' People had warned me that there was no shallow end to philosophy, but this seemed to be requiring us novices to enter the pool from a high diving board in the dark! I remember vividly, too, a wonderful series of seminars around the time that Michael Young's *Knowledge and Control* was published, when the philosophers descended *en bloc* to encounter the sociologists of knowledge, although on reflection I can't help feeling that these encounters created a false and enduring dichotomy in Britain between sociological and philosophical engagement with the nature and structure of knowledge, one which it has been part of my intention to erode in the context of educational research. After all, the idea that knowledge is socially constructed, the proposal that there is an intimate association between power and the validation of belief, the suggestion that justice and the right are socially relative are themselves *philosophical* notions with an extensive philosophical heritage. Socrates may have been convinced that he had demolished Thrasymachus's suggestion that 'Justice is nothing but the interests of the stronger man' (Richards, 1966: 21), but the proposition was nevertheless an acknowledged and provocative part of the philosophical debate and it continues to be so.

These happy recollections of my own career I offer not just in the spirit of the nostalgic reverie which anniversary occasions are wont to provoke, but because they continue to inform my own approach both to teacher education and to educational research.

Those entrusted with the mission of education must, I believe, be in touch with and draw on the richest, the most challenging and the most vigorous intellectual currents of their history and of their own day. If they are not, then the process of education itself becomes inert, pupils are sold short on an impoverished substitute for their proper intellectual inheritance and society institutionalizes intellectual obsolescence and torpor. This is one crucial reason why the universities must retain – or perhaps I should say recoup – a central place in the education of teachers and a central voice (or plurality of voices) in the conversations which inform their education.

A fortiori I shall argue these same intellectual currents, the big ideas which challenge, disturb, deepen and enrich our understanding need to inform the activities of educational research – and it is to this more specifically that I will turn shortly.

As a starting point, however, I think it is important to recognize what kind of a perspective the wider educational research community and the philosophy of education community seem to have of each other, because it is my concern that if philosophy of education is to receive the recognition it ought to have for its contribution to educational research, then it has some ground to make up.

The Educational Research Community and Philosophy of Education

The Economic and Social Research Council (ESRC) Working Party on 'Frameworks and Priorities for Research in Education', chaired by John Gray (now on the Teacher Training Agency (TTA) Board) and with the Director of the Institute of Education among its distinguished membership, acknowledged that research in the social sciences required 'theoretical advancement' if it was to sustain its rigour. It observed that:

> There have been times in recent years when the development of theory has either been seen as unfashionable or been pushed off many researchers' agendas by the pressures of short-term,

narrowly focused studies. Researchers in education need to keep abreast of developments elsewhere if they are to sustain the theoretical vigour of their enquiries and to impact, more generally, on the collective social science endeavour.

(Gray et al., 1998: 4)

This account of the outcomes of the Working Group's deliberations, like most recent statements of its kind, manages nevertheless to avoid a single utterance of that apparently embarrassing or forgotten word – philosophy!

Similarly, of five 'position papers' on Quality in Educational Research presented in a focal session to the 1994 British Educational Research Association (BERA) conference, only one makes reference to philosophy – and this is hardly an encouraging one. Gwen Wallace writes:

Educational researchers have broadly abandoned the academic disciplines of sociology, philosophy and psychology in favour of school or classroom-based studies. What distinguishes educational research is its relationship to practice.

(Wallace, 1994: 2, in Bassey et al., 1994)

David Hargreaves' influential 1996 TTA lecture (Hargreaves, 1996) made not a single reference to philosophy, but his enthusiastic endorsement of the 'evidence-based practice' currently fashionable (but also heavily critiqued) in the health service suggested in any case little enthusiasm for it. Perhaps inspired by Hargreaves' exhortations, David Blunkett recently called on the TTA 'to clamp down on' educational research which was not applied. He said 'Research has historically not been closely related to the improvement of classroom practice.... This must change' (*Times Higher Educational Supplement*, 1997: 2). So much for the academic freedom of the universities!

There are some influential figures in the research community who clearly recognize the importance, even the urgency, of the philosophical contribution. Stewart Ranson, for example, in a recent report to the ESRC under the title 'The future of education research: learning at the centre', argued that:

> The transformations of our time are altering the structure of experience and the powers and capacities needed to live in a post-modern world. The changes raise deep questions for education and for the polity in general about: what is it to be a person? ... Is there such a thing as society and what is it? ... What should be the nature of the polity?
>
> (Ranson, 1996: 11)

There is, however, something slightly strange about Ranson's argument, partly because he writes as if these questions were peculiarly associated with 'the post-modern world' and partly because he at no point acknowledges that there is in philosophy a discipline which has been dedicated for over 2,000 years to precisely such questions as these.

So, there are two problems here. The first concerns the marginalization of philosophy of education from the mainstream educational research community in this country. The second, if the Hargreaves and the Blunketts of this world get their way, is the threat of its very exclusion from that community on the grounds of its irrelevance to classroom practice.

The picture the other way round, that is in terms of the perspective of philosophers of education on the educational research community, has only recently become slightly more encouraging. Until the mid 1990s, there were probably no more than three or four members of the Philosophy of Education Society of Great Britain attending the annual BERA conference, and these were there largely by virtue of their involvement in research which was not primarily philosophical. *The British Educational Research Association Journal* has not to my knowledge published a single philosophical paper (probably because it has never been offered such material). However, things are changing. In 1996 and 1997 we were able to attract something like 120 philosophers and empirical researchers to one or more of the symposia we have established at the annual conference on the theme of philosophy and educational research, and these have been widely regarded as among the most stimulating events at the conference. In 1997, this programme was extended to the European Education Research Association conference in Frankfurt, at which Dietrich Lenzen (President of the German Philosophy of Education Society, which, interestingly, is an integral part of the German Educational Research Association) independently proposed the establishment of a Philosophy of Education Network and, again, found a very positive response. The Executives of both BERA and the Philosophy of Education Society of Great Britain have agreed on a formal association between the two societies in order to bring the two communities closer together.

All of this may be of little interest in strictly philosophical terms, but the lessons of those 1970s debates about the sociology of knowledge were not entirely wasted on me. I am afraid that philosophers of education, no less than any other academic community, will neglect the politics of the advancement, marginalization and suppression of different forms of discourse at their peril.

No doubt, however, one condition of moving from the margins to the mainstream of educational attention is for philosophers to be clearer and more promotional themselves as to what their discipline and subject has to offer and, more particularly in this instance, as to the relationship of philosophy to educational research. So let me contribute some thoughts on this.

Conceptual Analysis

The training I received at the Institute of Education was largely, although not exclusively, in the analytical tradition of philosophy which held that the analysis of the meaning of the language, in particular the central concepts that we employ in particular areas of discourse, was the key to resolving their obdurate problems and debates, or at least, more modestly, an essential prerequisite. This is a view of philosophy of education recently re-affirmed by John Wilson (Wilson, 1994 and 1998) and lucidly expounded in a paper by John and Patricia White presented to a seminar in Amsterdam (White and White, 1997).

I remain extremely positively disposed towards clarity in the use of language. I am sceptical of ideas presented in what sometimes seems to me an obscurantist language born out of intellectual idleness and inconsiderateness of the reader rather than profundity of thought, and I remain frustrated when I observe educational debates in which substantive issues are obscured or ignored because the participants are lost in a confusion of the meaning of the terms which they are employing. However, you do not need to be a philosopher to care about these things or to seek to address them in academic writing.

My own confidence in conceptual analysis as a philosophical tool has been undermined on a number of fronts.

First, there was always a slippery slope in the literature which employed the analytical approach which ran from *(a)* a supposedly neutral descriptive analysis of the way a particular concept was employed, through *(b)* a prescriptive recommendation of the way language ought to be used, to *(c)* a more or less heavily disguised prescription of what people ought to do or to value. This was well traced through the 1970s in critical commentary on, for example, Richard Peters' work on the concept of education. I will probably illustrate the same slipperiness shortly when I propose my own account of the philosophical.

Second, and perhaps more importantly, the business of conceptual analysis appeared increasingly problematic as philosophers, no less than any other researchers, were obliged to acknowledge certain features of language itself:

- the complexity and subtlety of the ways in which language in use acquires and conveys meaning;
- more specifically, the connotative and psycho-dynamic as well as the denotative meaning of words;
- the ways in which the meaning of words and phrases operate as a function of the particular social and cultural context in which they are employed;
- the way in which meaning is constructed interactively and negotiated in specific encounters between people;
- the ultimate reliance of people on an ability to understand language in use which does not depend on having resort to an analysis or

definition of the meaning of words (because the alternative is an infinite regress in search of definitions of definitions of definitions...).

My own view is that once you have acknowledged these five features of language in use you have fairly seriously undermined the more ambitious 1960s notions of the power of conceptual analysis as an intellectual tool, perhaps in favour of some forms of discourse analysis, although these themselves may embody some of the same problems and some different ones (for example, the apparent non-falsifiability of certain forms of textual analysis).

Third, of course, even on a much more optimistic account of the benefits which conceptual analysis might deliver it was never sufficient for the resolution of the great or even the more modest substantive philosophical issues. An analysis of the meaning of the word 'ought' was never going to tell us what kinds of things we ought or ought not to do. An analysis of the concept of 'teaching' was never going to tell us how to teach, although there were heady times in the 1970s when philosophers seemed to come close to believing that it would.

The Application of the Sub-disciplines of Philosophy to Educational Research

The most readily recognizable contributions which philosophy can make to educational research are to the kind of second order questions with which that community is itself extensively, and in my view extremely interestingly, engaged. I mean in particular the debates within that community rooted in theory of knowledge about:

- the place of the subjectivity of the researcher in research writing;
- the different kinds of inference, generalizability and validation involved in different kinds of research;
- the displacement of truth or 'Truth' as a criterion to which research might aspire;

- the status and character of different kinds of text incorporated in research reports.

I mean, too, debates rooted in ethics and politics about:

- the relationship between the researcher and the researched;
- the obligations of researchers to their audiences, to their sponsors and to a wider public;
- the rights of those participating in one way or another in the research process.

Barry MacDonald said recently that research 'is fiction written under oath. The only question is, "What's the oath?"' That was an off-the-cuff remark from an empirical researcher, but I confess I could not immediately come up with a more engaging philosophical question!

The positive observation here, which goes some way to counter the rather dismal picture that I presented of mainstream researchers' perspectives on philosophy of education, is that these are questions which a good number of educational researchers – notable among them I am happy to say several of my colleagues at the University of East Anglia – are engaged with actively and with some sophistication. However, philosophers of education are only slowly beginning to turn their attention to this fertile terrain.

Yet, it is also territory which many contributors to BERA, for example, safe perhaps in their assumption that they can get away with any sweeping philosophical statement without challenge, enter with a shameless disregard for elementary scholarship. I been dismayed at recent conferences to hear cavalier dismissals of 'the Enlightenment Project' by people who lack even the slightest first-hand acquaintance with any of the writing of 'Enlightenment' philosophers and some of whom I suspect would be pushed even to come up with their names. It has become routine for some kinds of educational researchers to dismiss the notion of truth or more strictly 'Truth', while continuing to present papers which clearly imply the truth of what they have to say and certainly ignore the consequences of their own assertion for the status of that very assertion. In rather the same way, researchers pronounce the social relativity of values and simultaneously the unambiguous wickedness of the oppression of, for example, women, blacks or gays without any sense of the way in which the one assertion might undermine the other. Philosophers would, I suggest, find something to contribute as well as something to excite them in participation in these events.

Philosophy, 'Big Ideas' and Educational Research

I feel, however, that to define the terrain of the philosophical simply in terms of its sub-disciplines and their disciplined and technical contribution to the kinds of questions with which researchers are concerned is to take too narrow a standpoint. Indeed, one of the problems which has beleaguered the development of philosophy and philosophy of education in the Anglo-Saxon world has been the determination of philosophers to show how they differ from sociologists, cultural theorists, historians, psychologists and political economists, not to mention natural scientists, rather than what they might have in common.

I wish, by contrast, to present philosophy as not so much a discrete discipline occupying a small corner of the intellectual life, but as the terrain on which all forms of thought encounter their most profoundly formative, and their most profoundly disruptive, ideas. On this account, the territory of the philosophical may be characterized in the following inter-connected ways.

First, the philosophical concerns those beliefs which, in Quinean terms, are most deeply 'entrenched' in our belief systems, 'where the degree of entrenchment measures the degree to which any particular belief is entwined with other beliefs' (Everitt and Fisher, 1995: 189). Some of these beliefs may have been established historically out of an *a priori* reflection on, for example, the nature of matter or of human experiencing. Others may as a matter of fact have arisen out of observation of the physical or social world. The story of how they happen to have come to be established does not, however, fix them forever as being of a particular and distinct logical character. They are different in the degree of their embeddedness and not by virtue of the particular kind of act of imagination or observation which will be necessary in the future for their disconfirming or their disruption.

Second, which perhaps follows, the philosophical is concerned with big ideas, that is seminal intellectual currents which typically run across politics, art, literature, economy, sociology, psychology, historiography, morality and science, or a wider rather than a narrower range of all these. Thus, the doctrine of the fall of man, the Copernican Revolution, the articulation of humanism, the 'Death of God' (whether announced prematurely or not), dialectic materialism, Darwinianism, the notion of the unconscious and the theory of relativity, have impinged on every corner of our intellectual lives, have changed the assumptions under which those lives are led, and thus rank as truly philosophical notions.

Third, the philosophical seeks to be synoptic and systematic. It aspires to 'a theory of everything', but, short of this, seeks a coherent perspective or mutually supportive set of perspectives across a range of issues.

Fourth, the philosophical is rooted in a rich historic literature which, notwithstanding its historicity, remains pertinent to contemporary analysis and debate – an enduring relevance which is perhaps a function of the fundamental or deeply embedded nature of the matters which it addresses. It is in this sense in the terrain of whatever is both most enduring and most universal.

Now it seems to me perfectly proper to expect that for much of the time educational research will be occupied with some of the nitty gritty and practical problems which arise in the context of the classroom, school or educational system. However, I would wish to argue that the thinking, the understanding, the imagination and the analytical frameworks which underpin even this kind of research need to be informed and constantly re-informed by reference to the philosophical as I have described it:

- by the critical re-examination of our more deeply embedded assumptions (after all if the educational research community is not going to do this, no-one else in education is);
- by the 'big ideas' which run across the wider intellectual culture (because educational research will otherwise ensure that it is trapped

in the trivial, starved of imagination and marginalized from the broader context of social science research and the broader streams of our intellectual life if it is not so informed);

- by working to achieve their coherence with a more synoptic vision of the world (because the test of coherence and consistency may be the nearest we can get to the truth);

- by the historic and contemporary literature through which these kinds of ideas are articulated (because to ignore this is perversely to prefer the puny resources of one's own imagination to the collective wealth and memory of humankind).

This means not only that researchers of all kinds need to be in touch with these 'philosophical' sources, but that those whose primary intellectual engagement is in this territory need to be reaching out to those engaged in education itself and to educational research *a fortiori*.

Philosophy, Educational Research and Educational Practice

I have been advancing the case for engagement with 'big ideas', with theory and with the philosophical in a variety of forms, but I would not wish this to be construed as an argument for detachment from practice.

> I cannot praise a fugitive and cloistered virtue, unexercised and unbreathed, that never sallies out and sees her adversary, but slinks out of the race, where the immortal garland is to be run for, not without dust and heat.
> (Milton, 1644, 1967 edn: 158)

Indeed, whatever my pleasure in the intrinsic delights of philosophy, my original and continued main reason for engaging with philosophy lies in my conviction of its capacity to enhance and inform the practice of education, and I believe that this remains the main rationale for philosophy of education as such and for the contribution which it makes to educational research.

There are perhaps two relationships here which need to be distinguished. First, philosophy can constitute itself an independent form of enquiry or research into *educational practice* by informing, enriching and critiquing it. Second, philosophy can contribute to other forms of *research into educational practice* by informing, enriching and challenging them. So far, I have dealt largely with the relationship between philosophy and other forms of educational research, so let me conclude with a few comments on the more direct relationship with educational practice in which philosophy itself constitutes the first order research activity or form of enquiry. I have always liked Passmore's notion of subjects as 'critico-creative traditions' (Passmore, 1970: 192-212) and it is helpful here to think of both the critical and the creative contributions of philosophy to educational practice.

In terms of its critical function, I offer the following observations.

First, that there are some limitations to what philosophy can handle in research terms. Philosophy cannot, for example, engage with behaviour, only with the beliefs which in fact underlie behaviour or, more conjecturally, may be attached to it in some way. However, it cannot engage with those beliefs if they remain tacit (hence, philosophy has difficulty in engaging with craft knowledge and tends to disparage it). It requires them to be made explicit. Furthermore, it requires them to be made explicit in a relatively formal way – essentially as a text which employs the language and concepts with which philosophers themselves are familiar.

What is interesting to observe is the way in which some of those who are working across the boundaries of philosophy and educational practice – I think of the work of Morwenna Griffiths in Nottingham (Griffiths, 1997) and Eileen Francis and her VECTOR circle in Edinburgh (Francis, 1997) – find themselves supporting just such articulation of teachers' practice by the teachers themselves, helping them to:

- express what is implicit;
- clarify the values and beliefs that underlie their practice;

- connect these with ideas available in the literature;
- join their professional language with this academic discourse.

It is sometimes difficult to escape in this kind of activity the picture of the philosopher playing Miranda to the teacher's Caliban: 'I endow'd thy purposes with words which made them known' (Shakespeare, *The Tempest*, Act 1, sc. 2). However, perhaps this reflects the essential dependency of the critical function of philosophical enquiry (and I am distinguishing this here from moral commentary, for example) on the articulation of practice in relatively sophisticated linguistic form.

Philosophy offers not only critique, but also creativity in the form of alternative vision, transformative ways of looking at the same phenomena or the same experience, constructs of what might be and pictures of a preferred world. The vision and the imagination with which educational research can inform educational practice are significantly a function of the vision and imagination which are brought to the research. It is intriguing to observe how some people in the educational research field manage to conjure exciting ideas out of very modest data, while others labour endlessly to demonstrate the predictable and the mundane. ('Rubbish in, rubbish out' as they say in data processing.)

The fruits of, for example, classroom action research over the last two decades have sometimes been exciting. Certainly, it has been a mode of research which has demonstrated a capacity to inform and to contribute to the development of practice. To a significant extent, however, it has pre-supposed in its practitioners, and even more in those that have supervised its practice, a familiarity with a rich and informing resource of theory and conceptual development which was rooted in earlier education in the disciplines of education. As, progressively, educational practitioners and educational researchers themselves enter their field of professional practice without experiencing either the rigour or the wide-ranging conceptual enrichment rooted in these disciplines, then I believe both educational practice and educational research will be deeply impoverished. Not only do few current modular MA programmes offer this kind of training, but the TTA's latest requirements for funded continuing professional development, which require that it all be couched in and assessed by reference to practical competence, promise to put the nails firmly in the coffin of a disciplined and theoretically informed approach to the in-service education of teachers within its domain for the foreseeable future.

So I urge those who define themselves as philosophers of education to unite with those who engage with the philosophical across all the domains of educational research in a determination to ensure that:

- political agencies do not confine educational research to an agenda which takes their policies as a given;
- bureaucratic agencies do not confine educational research to the pedestrian and mundane;
- the philistine and anti-intellectual voices inside as well as outside our school staffrooms do not confine the adventurous imaginations of the best of our educators and researchers only to the conditions of the here and now;
- educational research and practice is informed and challenged by the 'big ideas' and the most radical questions received from the past and generated across the full range of contemporary intellectual life.

Here, I believe, is the challenge for the *next* 50 years of philosophy and education at the Institute of Education, London, and in its sister institutions across the country in which philosophy of education continues to flourish, or at least manages to survive.

References

Bassey, M., Deem, R., Troyna, B., Harlen, W., Wallace, G. and Whitehead, J. (1994), 'Quality in educational research: position papers for a round-table discussion'. British Educational Research Association Annual Conference, Oxford, 10 September.

Everitt, N. and Fisher, A. (1995), *A Modern Epistemology*. New York: McGraw Hill.

Francis, E. (1997), 'Developing the philosophical voice in educational research'. Paper presented to the annual conference of the British Educational Research Association, York, September.

Gray, J., Black, P., Brown, S., Burgess, R., Constable, H., Deem, R., Driver, R., Gibson, A., Light, P., Mortimore, P., Murphy, R., Pollard, A., Phoenix, A., Spencer, E. and De Vries, P. (1998) 'Frameworks and priorities for research in education: towards a strategy for the ESRC' in MacIntyre, A. and Rudduck, J. (eds), *The Future of Educational Research*. Edinburgh: BERA.

Griffiths, M. (1997), 'Why teachers and philosophers need each other: philosophy and educational research', *Cambridge Journal of Education*, 27(2), 191-202.

Hargreaves, D.H. (1996), *Teaching as a Research-based Profession: Possibilities and Prospects*. Teacher Training Agency Annual Lecture, London: Teacher Training Agency.

Milton, J. (1967 edn), 'Areopagitica' in *Milton's Prose Writings*. London: Dent (Everyman's Library).

Passmore, J. (1967), 'On teaching to be critical' in Peters, R.S. (ed.), *The Concept of Education*. London: Routledge.

Ranson, S. (1996), 'The future of education research: learning at the centre' in MacIntyre, A. and Rudduck, J. (eds), *The Future of Educational Research*. Edinburgh: BERA.

Richards, I.A. (1966), *Plato's Republic*. Cambridge: Cambridge University Press.

Times Higher Education Supplement (1997), 'Blunkett calls for more applied research', 31 October, 2.

Young, M.F.D. (1971), *Knowledge and Control*. London: Collier-Macmillan.

White, J. and White, P. (1997), 'Analytic philosophy of education and children's rights'. Paper presented to seminar on Philosophical Method, University of Amsterdam, October.

Wilson, J. (1994), 'Philosophy and educational research: first steps'. Paper presented to annual conference of British Educational Research Association, Oxford, September.

— (1998), 'Philosophy and educational research: a reply to David Bridges et al.', *Cambridge Journal of Education*, 28(1).